University of Washington Publications on Asian Arts
SPONSORED BY THE CENTER FOR ASIAN ARTS

A Jatra actor

Balwant
Gargi

FOLK
THEATER
OF
INDIA

University of Washington Press
Seattle and London

Endpapers: (front) the battle between the ogress Taraka and Rama and Lakshmana, as the bearded guru Vishwamitra blesses them; (back) the chase of the Golden Deer. A nineteenth-century kalamkari (painting on cloth) from the wall of a South Indian temple. Courtesy of the National Museum, New Delhi

Copyright © 1966 by the University of Washington Press
Library of Congress Catalog Card Number 66–19558
Printed in the United States of America
Designed by Audrey Meyer

"When I come onto the stage, Shakti, the Goddess of Power, sits on my face, and Saraswati, the Goddess of Learning, on my tongue."

—Saying of a folk actor

FOREWORD

THE CENTER for Asian Arts at the University of Washington has sponsored the publication of this study on the Indian folk theater as the first of a series dealing with various aspects of the arts of Asia. Although Far Eastern studies are now being encouraged in a growing number of colleges and universities in this country, little has been done to promote a systematic study of Asian arts. Such studies as do exist in this field are usually appendages for the enrichment of curricula whose primary emphases are placed, both traditionally and logically, on Western culture. The time has come to undertake a closer examination of the various art forms of Asia with comparative horizontal investigations embracing all of the arts of a given period. These investigations, in juxtaposition with the values, concepts, and methods indigenous to Western arts, will bring fresh insights and a new perspective to the study and understanding of Western culture.

The folk theater of India, as described in Balwant Gargi's study, offers excellent material for horizontal investigations since it combines elements of literature, performance, dance, and music with aspects of painting and sculpture as expressed in costumes, masks, make-up, and settings. Mr. Gargi completed his basic text in India before he came to the University of Washington as a guest of the Center. While in residence here, Mr. Gargi has not only lectured on this subject, but has been able to test his theories in practice. Using American students as actors, Mr. Gargi has produced classical and modern plays in Indian folk form for an English-speaking audience with great success.

Further investigations of other Asian theatrical traditions are being sponsored by the Center, and the results are planned for subsequent volumes of the series.

MILLARD B. ROGERS
Director, Center for Asian Arts

PREFACE

INDIAN folk theater has recently captured the interest of contemporary playwrights and directors. The city theater, modeled on the nineteenth-century picture-frame stage, has little new to offer; the classical dance-dramas with their thick-textured music and gesture language are esoteric. It is the folk theater lying scattered in rural areas of India which has exciting forms. These forms, perfected during the centuries by constant adjustment to social changes, have been evolved by actual battling with the needs of the audience and the actors.

My search for the various types of folk theater took me to far-flung villages, shrines, country fairs, and tribal areas where people still dance and mime animal hunts by torchlight. Of the many forms, I have chosen the nine which seem to me most fully developed.

Folk theater is a popular form of entertainment; therefore scholars have not thought it worthy of serious consideration. Almost no books are available on the subject. Actual performances in their natural settings were my guide. Not knowing the language in most areas, I was handicapped on a literary level, but this heightened my theatrical perception since all my understanding was derived from the acting, dancing, music, and stylized projection. Masks, make-up, and costumes added another important dimension. The performances gave me a chance to become acquainted with the history, life, customs, beliefs, rituals, music, landscape, and the particular background which gave rise to these powerful forms.

In my discussion of the plays I have tried to give literal translations of the titles except when this was merely the name of a character or a place. At times a word or a phrase has been added to make the meaning clearer to the English reader.

I am grateful to many friends, chance acquaintances, actors, singers, costume makers, and dancers who were hospitable to me in areas where I was unfamiliar with the language. These performers and friends have been my "reference book." I am especially indebted to the following: Shivaram Karanth, who toured the coastal villages of North Kanara with me and guided me in the understanding of Yakshagana music and its ritualistic conventions (his collection of palm-leaf manuscripts was particularly helpful in tracing the tradition); Keshavrao Bhole for explaining the aesthetics of drumming and lavani singing in Tamasha; Sharman Lal Aggarwal and Bharat Bhushan Aggarwal for guiding me to shrines and holy places in the Braj area, where we "temple-crawled" sampling Raslila performances; Banda Kankalingeshwar Rao for taking me to Kuchipudi village to see the art of the gurus; Amar Nath Pathak and Arati Pathak for accompanying me to rural Bengal and interpreting plays night after night; Dr. Suresh Awasthi for helping me see the Nautanki in different styles; Dr. Bhanushankar for leading me in Varanasi streets to the cycle plays about Rama's life; the Maharaja of Banaras for opening the royal archives and supplying me with a troupe of pundits to read and explain the manuscripts; Rajkumar Suddhendra of Seraikella for giving metaphysical interpretations of the Chhau masks and the background of jewelry, costume, and themes; Janakiraman for throwing sidelights on the Therukoothu; Dina Gandhi and Amritlal Jeevaram Naik Pansarwala for artistic demonstrations that made the Bhavai form more vivid to me; Shanta Kirloskar, my hostess in Poona, who helped me to grasp the cultural and historical background of Maharashtra; and the elderly blind S. G. Gore, the patron of Tamasha troupes, who was my guide at actual performances.

I also wish to express my gratitude to Dr. V. Raghavan and Ralph Berens, who went through the manuscript and chastened it, and to Mohan Khokar for his extremely valuable suggestions.

Shiavax Chavda deserves my special gratitude as his line drawings have added charm to my written word. All photographs, unless otherwise indicated, are my own.

This book was made possible by the sponsorship of the Punjabi University, Patiala. I am grateful to Bhai Jodh Singh for his personal interest in this research project. I am also thankful to the Asia Foundation, the Ministry of Education of India, the Punjab Government, and the Center for Asian Arts of the University of Washington for their grants.

BALWANT GARGI

CONTENTS

Folk Theater of India

Chapter One

THE FOLK
AND THE
CLASSICAL

THE FOLK theater is impolite, rude, vulgar. It shocks prudes. The secular forms—Tamasha, Bhavai, Nautanki, and Naqal —dominating the northern and western parts of India are replete with sexual jokes. It is considered improper for women to watch these plays. In the city of Poona, many professors and intellectuals, champions of culture, refuse to see a folk play because of its "vulgarity."

Folk drama is unself-conscious, spontaneous, boisterously naïve. The classical theater is rigid, complex, sophisticated. The folk is unhewn, the classical chiseled. The folk sprawls, the classical demands mathematical exactness. One is rural, the other regal.

Folk theater can make a whole community take part; the classical is for the chosen few. The folk has mass appeal and caters to the lowest common denominator, the ordinary man; the classical is for the elite and demands previous knowledge from the spectator. The folk theater has a universality which the classical lacks. Folk art (singing, dancing, acting) crosses the borders of class, religion, and country. The classical often imposes these barriers because of its esoteric nature.

The relationship between the classical and folk theater is complex. They are not antitheses of each other. They coexist; they borrow and lend. We know that folk art always precedes classical. Cave drawings and primitive hunt mimes were the precursors of painting and dancing. Greek tragedy and comedy were born out of fertility rites and the frenzied worship of Dionysus. The classical Indian drama also grew out of pageants, rituals, mimes, and ancient folk forms. But the Indian folk theater prevalent in rural areas today is only four to six hundred years old.

India is a country of kaleidoscopic contrasts. Four hundred and eighty million people inhabit the giant triangle which stretches from the snow-capped Himalayas down to the tapering tropical Cape Comorin. There are fifteen major languages, including English; more than seven hundred dialects; six im-

portant religions; half a dozen ethnic groups; and many different castes and creeds. The wheat-complexioned bearded Sikhs in their colored turbans in the Punjab; the ebony-bodied naked Santhals in the east; the close-shaven Dravidian priests of the south; the full-busted dark women of Maharashtra; the Mongolian-flavored people of Assam; and the sun-baked ballad singers of Rajasthan offer a baffling variety. Religious beliefs, eating habits, social customs, rituals, styles of turbans, hairdos, and beards, and the draping of saris and dhotis differ from region to region. Yet the people are bound by a common impulse embedded in their philosophy, music, arts, and tradition. The folk theater mirrors both this variety and this unity.

When, after the tenth century, the classical Sanskrit language splintered into vernaculars and took root in the form of regional languages, the Sanskrit drama—petrified for many centuries—was replaced by the growing folk theater. Old legends, Puranic tales, mythological lore, philosophy, and stories of Sanskrit plays were popularized by the present folk theater. In this way the tradition flowed not from the folk to the classical, but from the classical to the folk.

The folk theater inherits many of the classical conventions.

The Sutradhara (Stage Manager) of Sanskrit drama appears in vernacular folk forms as the Ranga, the Bhagavatha, the Vyas, or the Swami. The Buffoon, the counterpart of the classical Vidushaka, is the darling of the folk theater. He appears under different names in various regional forms: Konangi,

Komali, Hanumanayaka, Joothan Mian. He speaks in rustic prose or dialect. He has the freedom to connect the past with the present and relate the drama to the contemporary scene. He also acts as liaison between the audience and the players. The *purvaranga* (stage preliminaries) is an essential feature of both Sanskrit and folk theater. The musicians take their positions on the stage, tune their instruments, and play a melody; the dancers perform a few dance numbers; the cast sings a *mangalacharana* (a vernacular form of the classical invocation). Some of the folk theaters also use a benediction at the end of the play. They employ music, dance, stylization, verse dialogue, exaggerated make-up, and masks with the same lavishness as the classical drama. Scenes melt into one another. The action continues in spite of changes of locale and scene. Asides, soliloquies, and monologues abound.

Folk theater represents the people in their natural habitat, with all their contradictions and multifarious activities. It gives a glimpse of their style of speech, music, dance, dress, behavior, humor, proverbs, wit, and wisdom. It contains a rich store of mythological heroes, medieval romances, chivalric tales, social customs, beliefs, and legends. In order to understand the colorful diversity and unity of India, it is important to see the folk theater in its natural setting. Watching a Tamasha performance in Maharashtra, one comes to know more about the Peshwas, the Maratha heroism, their rugged landscape, their music, their passionate optimism, their dogged

virility, and the full-busted female figures of their cave sculpture. Similarly the Gangetic Valley culture, philosophy, and traditional morality are mirrored in Ramlila and Krishnalila pageant plays. Yakshagana, the opulent folk opera of Kanara land, reveals the tradition, temple worship, and the peculiar music and ritual of its people. The Jatra of Bengal expresses patriotic fervor, histrionic refinement, and explosive nationalism with an interlacing of the Vaishnava cult.

The folk theater does not give a slice of life; it offers a panorama of existence. Though it moves slowly, it cannot afford to be dull. The spectators are participants in the performance. They cheer and laugh and weep and suddenly become silent as the moment demands. They constantly throw sparks of live interest to the actors who, charged with this electrifying contact, throw the spark back. A good Yakshagana company can hold spectators spellbound from nine in the evening to seven in the morning when the play concludes with the first shafts of the sun. Jatra actors in Bengal are a bigger draw than modern professional actors. A good Jatra company generally has a salaried staff of 15,000 rupees* per month (one actor, Chhota Phani, is paid 3,300 rupees a month) and performs without a microphone before an audience of three to five thousand people. The Jatra, in its production method, in its use of stage areas, movement, speed, and the oaklike stance of its actors, paradoxically looks more modern in terms of theatrical aesthetics than the realistic "modern" play.

Life in India is in the street. Shops, stalls, rituals, bathrooms are exposed to the sun and to the glare of the people. So is the folk theater.

The idea of a closed theater is almost foreign to the Indian masses. In the nineteenth century, when the British introduced their educational system, they also brought in the concept of the picture-frame stage. In big cities where the amateur movement developed, a few theater halls were built in mid-Victorian style with plush curtains, gilded chairs, and chandeliers. But in seven hundred thousand villages of India the traditional dance-dramas, pageants, operatic ballads, and folk plays continue to entertain audiences in the open air.

The folk play is performed in a variety of arena stagings: round, parabolical, horizontal, square, and multiple-set stages, with different types of gangways and "flower paths." The technique of arranging various scenes at the same time and place in Ramlila is very effective. The spectacle, by the telescoping of time and space, speeds the action of the drama. The naked stage achieves spacelessness. The Sutradhara, like a film editor,

* One dollar equals approximately 4.75 rupees.

builds up a montage of varied dramatic episodes. The same spot is transformed into a different place by a word or an action. The folk actor uses very few props. He creates palaces, rivers, forests, battle scenes, and royal courts by the sorcery of his art.

The most crystallized folk theater forms are: Jatra of Bengal; Nautanki, Ramlila, and Raslila of North India; Bhavai of Gujarat; Tamasha of Maharashtra; Therukoothu of Tamilnad; Yakshagana of Kanara; and the Chhau mask dramas of Seraikella. These forms give a glimpse of the richness of folk theater and folk culture and the passion of the people for life and drama.

India

JAMMU & KASHMIR

• Srinagar

HP

HIMACHAL PRADESH

• Simla

Chandigarh

PUNJAB

New Delhi

UTTAR

• Mathura

PRADESH

Jaipur •

RAJASTHAN

• Lucknow
• Varanasi

SIKKIM
Gangtok •

BHUTAN

NEFA

ASSAM

Shillong •

NAGALAND

Imphal •

MANIPUR

• Patna

BIHAR

Agartala •

TRIPURA

WEST BENGAL

GUJARAT

Ahmedabad •

• Bhopal

MADHYA PRADESH

• Calcutta

ORISSA

• Bhubaneswar

MAHARASHTRA

BAY OF BENGAL

Bombay •

• Poona

• Hyderabad

MYSORE

ANDHRA PRADESH

GOA

KANARA LAND

ARABIAN SEA

Bangalore •

• Madras

• Pondicherry

KERALA

MADRAS

Trivandrum •

Chapter Two

JATRA

A JATRA actor can be recognized by the way he stands—a tilted tower. He does not hold himself back but throws his weight forward. Passionate, charged with energy, he explodes into fiery dialogue. He moves like a tornado in the small arena. In spite of continuous action, he has a firm grip on the ground.

THE STAGE

A two-and-a-half-foot raised platform sixteen feet square is the stage, the asar. The orchestra is seated on two ramps, each six inches lower than the platform and running parallel on opposite sides. On one side are the percussion players with drums, cymbals, and bells. The other side holds the flutist, violinist, clarinetist, harmonium player, and two trumpeters. Huge bulbs, fastened to four poles pitched at the four corners of the asar, illuminate the stage and the sweat-soaked faces of the spectators. The women sit on one side, as in temple gatherings; the men squat on the other three sides. The boys huddle near the rim of the stage. Strings of lights run diagonally across the canopied arena. Here and there neon tubes throw bluish gleams.

The only property on the stage is a chair. This can represent a throne, a bench, a log of wood, a prisoner's seat, a tower. Women going to bathe in a river put their clothes on it, and it becomes the steps of the ghat. Other properties are brought in and removed by the actors themselves. If dramatic necessity requires, a stagehand seated among the musicians saunters up the asar, picks up the properties, and disappears.

A gangway, bordered by short bamboo strips and thin ropes, runs from one corner of the stage to the dressing room, sixty feet away, which is embellished with a silk curtain bearing the name of the company in red and gold script. Through this gangway the actor enters and exits. At important moments it becomes a part of the acting area. If the heroine separates from her lover, she walks haltingly down the gangway speaking her last lines. If a comedian-servant is spurned by his master, he makes his unwilling exit through the gangway, making the audience roar at every step as he whines and gibbers. The gangway can serve as street, or temple path, or highway. Marriage parties, funeral processions, and armies march down it. Standing on this gangway the Vivek, a stage character representing the Conscience, sings out the inner conflict of a character and warns him of impending doom. Theatrically he gives the play another dimension by being on a different spatial level. His words assume a foreboding note, as if voiced in a dream—a whisper that has a terrifying clarity.

The gangway is in some respects reminiscent of the hana-michi (flower path) of the Kabuki theater of Japan, a four-

11

foot-wide polished wood path, flanked by small lights, that runs from the stage proper through the spectators to the back of the auditorium. Important entries and exits are made through it. It is an extension of the rectangular stage and at times serves as another acting area. At climactic moments the actor stands on it and strikes a pose—a *mie*—which in film terms would be a close-up. The Jatra gangway in some ways serves the same function.

Sometimes while the actor is on the gangway, visually and psychologically present, his exit is overlapped by the entry of another actor who immediately becomes engaged in action on the stage. This overlapping gives the Jatra performance con-

tinuity. The actors do not have to disappear completely in the wings as in Western representational theater.

BACKGROUND

Though the Jatra form is equally popular in Orissa and the eastern parts of Bihar (two bordering states), it originated in Bengal—the land of paddy fields, boatmen, saint-poets, Western industrialization, and social and political upheavals. The mighty Ganges, shooting from the Himalayas, sweeps down the plains and nurtures Bengal until it lazes into the bay. The monsoons burst and the rivers swell and the dark oily heat steams. The climate, soil, and people have a moist richness.

The men are swarthy; the women are known for their luxurious black hair and shining black eyes. Their songs, dances, and poetry have the gentle rhythm of swaying fields. The towns and cities have developed a middle class with an intellectual edge which is characterized by the strong impulse of their tradition, language, and folk culture.

In the fifteenth century, when the Bhakti movement swept Bengal, devotees went singing and dancing in processions. They sang in temple courtyards, narrating the events of their patron god's life, and expressed their devotion with frenzied acting. The collective singing amidst the clang of gongs and fumes of incense produced a mass hypnosis and sent these singers into an acting trance. This singing with dramatic elements gradually came to be known as "Jatra," which means "to go in a procession."

No record has been found of the earliest Jatra performance. Pundits differ on the etymology and interpretation of the word. Some quote ancient scriptures to link Jatra with the *Natyasastra* (the two-thousand-year-old holy book of dramaturgy ascribed to Bharata Muni) or to some dim distant event. They spend more time debating the age and date of Jatra than trying to understand the aesthetics of this spectacle which dominates Bengal's rural areas and city squares, electrifying the spectators with an almost insane theatrical pleasure.

Of many controversial interpretations, one by Phani Bhushan Bidyabinod, the celebrated sixty-eight-year-old actor-director-writer, claims that the Jatra concept grew out of the musical enactment of an episode in Lord Krishna's life: Krishna is leaving his foster parents and milkmaids in the woods of Vrindaban to start for Mathura in order to punish his uncle King Kamsa. His march or *jatra* to Mathura has been celebrated in the *palas* (plays), and this heart-rending separation became the favorite theme of singers and players. Later any *pala* about Krishna's life or about any other mythological hero was called Jatra.

The Vaishnava saint Chaitanya Deb (1485–1533), who preached the equality of man and the fraternity of the higher and lower castes, went into religious ecstasy as he sang and danced in the streets with his followers. His disciple, Chandra Sekhar, describes in his master's biography how one day Chaitanya Deb decided to perform *Rukmini Haran* ("The Abduction of the Charming Rukmini") from Krishna's life story, and asked his follower Sadashiva Buddhimanta Khan to make arrangements, paying particular attention to the make-up and costumes of the different characters. Special emphasis was laid on bangles, blouses, silken saris, ornaments. Chaitanya played Rukmini, Krishna's wife. His transformation was so complete

"that nobody could make out that she is Master himself!"*
Chaitanya Deb added to the existing Jatra the elements of
make-up and costume.

Popular forms of dramatic singing and expressive acting from
the sixteenth through the eighteenth century were: Jhumur
(duet songs with a bit of dance and dialogue), Panchali (a
performance by a single actor-singer), Kathakata (one actor
singing a religious story), Keertan (devotional singing), and
Kabigan (recitation). These were tributaries that flowed into
the Jatra form and enriched it.

In the eighteenth century Jatra had a sweeping popularity.
Famous *pala* writers on the Krishna theme included Parmanand Sen, a contemporary of Bharat Chandra (the late eighteenth-century poet who composed the famous *Bidya Sundar*
poetic romance); the two brothers Sreedan Das and Subol
Das; the singer-actor Badan Adhikari; and Sisuram Adhikari,
a Brahmin by caste, who brought structural perfection to the
Jatra. The masses were hungry for this intensely emotional
musical form. Those who did not believe in the Krishna cult
were fed on Rama, Shiva, and the goddess Kali. These *palas*
were called Rama Jatra, Shiva Jatra, and Chandi Jatra. Historical romances and love stories were added to the repertoire.
The most famous was *Bidya Sundar*, the story of Princess
Bidya and Prince Sundar, which started a new trend in the
Jatra. Many people wrote Bidya Sundar *palas*. These included
passionate scenes of abduction, murder, and horror.

By the close of the eighteenth century Bengal was completely under the East India Company. The last ruler of
Bengal, Nawab Siraj-ud-Daula, was defeated in 1757. The
British introduced permanent land settlements and a new
system of government. The rising gentry was prosperous.
Riches flowed, and with the new wealth came the desire for
entertainment. The gentry of Bengal invited the Jatra troupes
for such festive occasions as the Ratha Puja and Durga Puja
celebrations.

In the nineteenth century the Jatra repertoire swelled with
love themes, erotic stories, mythological heroes, historical romances, tales of legendary robbers, saints, social reformers,
and champions of truth and justice, diluting its religious color.
The Jatra became secular and more contemporary in character.
As political consciousness grew, Jatra writers gave political
coloring to their *palas*. Mythological stories, fights between
Good and Evil, symbolized the Indian masses and the British.

---

* The play was performed in Chandra Sekhar's house. The performance, which lasted throughout the night, is described in detail in *Chaitanya
Bhagavata* by Brindabanadasa Thakur. This is the first historically known
instance of a performance of Bengali Jatra.

The guru beseeches Debi, the wife of his disciple Ruidas in Petiter Bhagawan. (Right) *The guru on his knees beside Debi*

The Devil was dressed in the tight trousers and black jacket of the nineteenth century, and the Noble Prince wore the Indian dhoti.

Until the beginning of the twentieth century, the written text of a Jatra was in song and verse. In actual production, the Adhikari (Stage Manager) introduced prose bits. The actors spoke improvised dialogue. Scenes of humor and the life of the lower strata were in spicy prose. Still music and song dominated. There were easily fifty to sixty songs in a Jatra, which started in the afternoon and lasted till sunrise. Among the famous nineteenth-century Jatrawalas was Brajamohan Roy, who formed his Jatra troupe in 1872 and died four years later at the age of forty-five, leaving behind a number of successful plays, including *Ramabhisek* ("King Rama's Coronation"). Another famous Jatrawala of the period was the playwright-actor Motilal Roy, who introduced new energy into the acting style during the last quarter of the nineteenth century. Roy (a contemporary of Girish Ghosh, the founder of the professional Bengali stage) toured Bengal with his Jatra troupe, carrying forward the tradition.

Jatra underwent changes in every period—thematically and musically—but it retained its special flavor. With the advent of films and the growth of a powerful realistic acting tradition in the professional theater, Jatra suffered a setback. More and more prose was being used in the *palas*. The form fell into disrepute because of excessive use of murder, horror, and erotic elements. The vulgarity of the comic scenes was condemned by the middle class, the leaders of the Bengali intellectual revolution. Realistic portrayals of life in films with songs and dances fed the music-hungry audiences and partially replaced their lust for Jatra.

But Jatra never died in the rural areas. Even in Calcutta where it was suppressed, it cropped up at night in various squares and alleys. There is hardly a Bengali who in his boyhood has not sat for hours watching the colorful Jatra.

Today a Jatra *pala*, lasting four hours, consists of action-

packed dialogue with only six to eight songs. Still it retains its musical character. People wait for the songs, which in their popularity compete with those from films. Among the people the form retains its name "jatragan," which means "musical Jatra." When a Bengali goes to see a performance he says that he is going to "listen to" a Jatra. The actor who delivers monumental prose speeches says that he is going to "sing a Jatra."

The main play is preceded by preliminaries.

The musicians sitting on opposite sides of the asar start with a classical evening melody—sham kalyan, bihag, or poorbi. This orchestral piece, longer than the one that follows, is the "first concert." After a few minutes the musicians start the "second concert," a light, tripping melody which warns the actors and the audience that the play is about to begin. A quick musical flourish ends the concert, and a group of boys dressed like girls streams in from the gangway and begins to dance. If the actors are still busy making up, the group dance is followed by a solo dance.

After this comes an episode from the life of Krishna, or Shiva, or the goddess Durga. A popular pattern is the following. A Demon worshiping Shiva sits in yogic meditation. Shiva is pleased and grants a boon. The power-drunk Demon gets up to destroy the world, including Shiva himself. Many gods come one by one to defeat the Demon, but he is unconquerable. Ultimately the goddess Durga appears and kills the Demon. The fight ends in a tableau. Durga, with her ten hands, her gory tongue sticking out, stands triumphant astride her tiger. The other gods freeze into a silent action picture.

This piece includes acrobatics, sword fighting, wrestling, and feats of jumping and tumbling. It serves as a ritual of the triumph of Good over Evil and blesses the players and the spectators.

In earlier times the stage was at ground level. Slowly it developed into a two-and-a-half-foot-high raised platform so that the squatting masses could see the arena and the foot movements. The actors speak rapidly. There is seldom need for prompting, but a prompter sits on the ground on one edge of the arena, and in between the long dialogues he whispers a word here and there. He is a safety net. In his large handwritten manuscript songs are generally inscribed in Indian red, the names of the dramatic characters in bold vermilion, and the text in blue ink.

The play always starts with a climax. At the time when the audience may be bored by the long preliminaries, the boys scrambling for a good seat, and women gossiping, it takes a powerful stroke to alert them.

A Puranic play might start with the entry of a demon holding

The actor playing the Demon in Bhuler Mashool has painted teeth
on his upper lip

a dripping head. The historical *Samrat Zahandarshah* ("The Emperor Zahandarshah") opens with the firing of a gun. *Bargi Elo Deshe* ("The Maratha Invasion of Bengal") begins with the invaders looting the people. *Neel Kothi* ("The Oppression of Indigo Planters") opens with the plantation owners whipping the farm laborers. *Banglar Bodhu* ("The Bride of Bengal") starts with two groups quarreling over a disputed land. The Jatra playwright knows that the people must be dazzled, struck, shocked by a big event in the opening and not slowly taken from a low pitch to a high. The climactic beginning silences the murmuring crowd.

THE ACTOR

The Jatra actor has a sense of composition and speech delivery. He is superbly aware of the four-sided audience and is sturdily graceful from all angles. There is speed, action, flamboyance.

Sharp turns in mood, abrupt flares and sudden drops in pathos are underlined by the orchestra. Drums clatter and thump and rumble. The trumpeters blow, and the flute player weaves a tapestry of notes suiting the occasion. Background music, which the Bengali films introduced in the thirties, has long been a specialty of Jatra. The singing is always done by the actor and not by the musicians. In this the Jatra differs from most folk theaters where the Swami or the Ranga or the Bhagavatha or the Ramayani sing the lines for the actor and sometimes repeat the song for him. This is perhaps because in Yakshagana, Veedhi-natakam, and Tamasha the actors are required to do a great deal of dancing, which is at times so vigorous that they are out of breath and must be represented by the singing chorus. They may also be engaged in *abhinaya* (expressive miming) which requires the singer to tell the story and comment. In Jatra today, the function of the chorus or singing voices has been suspended.

Every actor does his own make-up. In the dressing room—a thatched enclosure three times larger than the stage—the actors sit cross-legged in rows with their make-up boxes. Glittering garments, silken saris, laced tunics, and wigs of many shapes and colors hang on the clothes line. The figure of the patron god or goddess, generally Krishna or Durga, is present, lighted by a small earthen lamp fed by ghee.

The actors use white lead, amber grease, and lamp soot to give an oily sheen to the face. Demons, brutal generals, and villains have intricate designs. Black stripes, crisscross lines, red streaks, and white knobs transform the actor into a fiendish character. His exterior is so awesome that it seems to be unreal. This gruesome unreality makes the spectator constantly conscious of the presence of a theatrical reality.

The use of make-up is ingenious. In the Navaranjan Opera Company the actor playing the Demon in the preliminaries of *Bhuler Mashool* ("Punishment for an Error") snarls and gnashes his teeth during a sword fight. His upper lip is painted with white teeth, and as he purses his lip and squints his eyes in pain, the painted lip looks like a set of teeth bared in a groan. The Cobbler Saint in the Natta Company's *Petiter Bhagawan* ("God of the Fallen") is played by the young actor Swapan Kumar Mukherjee. His spiked beard is a painted pattern of ink-black streaks. This austere nonrealistic make-up achieves power, boldness, and concentration.

The actors come from all classes—farmers, laborers, fishermen, clerks, peddlers, middle-class businessmen. In this respect Jatra is unlike the folk theater of Tamasha, Bhavai, Therukoothu, and Raslila, in which the profession of actor is hereditary and confined to special castes.

Traditionally, all roles have been played by male actors. Some play young heroes, some vicious villains, some comic fools, some the Vivek (Conscience), and some specialize in female roles. Recently some women have also joined the Jatra companies.

The tradition of having men play the parts of women is common in the Asian theater and commands respect. The *onnagata* of Japan have evolved over three centuries a stage woman that is impossible for the best Japanese actress to replace. In the Peking Opera Dr. Mei-lan Fang set the style of the graceful Chinese woman. Thirty years ago Peking women went to see Mei-lan Fang to copy his female grace. In India the leading male player of female roles during the twenties was Bal Gandharv, now eighty years old, who has been honored throughout Maharashtra for his services to the Marathi stage. Jayashankar Sundari of the Gujarati stage was also highly praised as a female type. Padmeshri Sthanam Narasimharao of Andhra was envied by women for his female charm and sex appeal. Talking about his memorable role of Moghul Emperor Aurangzeb's daughter, who disguised herself as a prince to go to the enemy court, he said: "While playing the young princess I effaced my identity and was a complete woman. But when I changed my garb and disguised myself as a prince, the natural thing for me would have been to be completely the young prince—easier for me since I am a man. But no. I had to be three persons at the same time. While playing the part of the handsome prince I retained the lyrical suppleness of the princess to show that in reality this was the princess in disguise. I had to be myself, the prince, and the princess."

The tradition resulted from the feudal social order in which

Sunil Roy (Satadal Rani) playing the bewitching heroine in Bhuler Mashool

women were kept in a lower place. In Japan and China, up to the time of World War II, women were considered inferior to men. Manu, the ancient supreme lawgiver of the Hindus, emphasized that a woman was never the equal of man. After the Muslims conquered India in the thirteenth century the position of women deteriorated further. For centuries women have been cloistered and not allowed to appear on the stage, while the men who played female roles developed a highly stylized interpretation of women. Today, although women are accepted in the theater, they find it difficult to adjust their own femaleness to the stylized "woman" of Jatra, and men are still the best "women" in Jatra.

Because of revolutionary social changes in the theater and films, the common man demands a woman actress to play the female roles; the urban middle class is completely taken over by the image of the glamorous actress. The Jatra male "actress" must fight a hard battle, depending solely upon his mastery of the art of acting. Many Jatra troupes now admit dancers, courtesans, and film extras, but none of these has become a star actress. It is difficult for a woman's voice to reach a crowd of five thousand spectators, whereas the male "actress" is trained to speak in falsetto without sounding harsh. In some Jatra companies there are mixed casts: of seven "female" players, three may be men and four women. The leading lady, however, is always played by a male.

The director-producer Surya Dutta of the Natta Company, a shriveled old man of eighty-four, has spent sixty-six years in the Jatra. Discussing the aesthetics of acting, he said: "It is no art if a woman plays a woman. When we represent a lame or cross-eyed man, we do not import a cripple or a cross-eyed man onto the stage. Theatrical enjoyment lies in the fact that an able-bodied man is limping and squinting. The natural thing is not the natural thing on the stage. When a man acts as a woman it is art!"

Hari Gopal Das, thirty-two, is the best emotional "actress." In the role of Debi, wife of the cobbler saint Ruidas in *Petiter Bhagawan*, he plays a victimized woman with voluptuous charm. He has twenty years of experience behind his feminine grace and wifely pathos. After watching the show I went into the dressing room where the actors were removing their beards and thick make-up. Hari Gopal Das was introduced to me. He still looked the bewitching wife. He held out his hand and I shook it, but when I wanted to embrace him, in appreciation of his art, I became embarrassed because he looked so stunningly feminine.

Most actors add the suffix *Rani* (graceful lady) to their name to distinguish themselves as female artists. Subal Mahanta, a farmer of Midnapur who was a star "actress" twenty years ago, was known by his feminine name Subal Rani. Shyamapade Chakravarty styles himself Chhabi Rani, and Sunil Roy, who plays an amorous princess or a coquettish wife, is famous as Satadal Rani. These actors do not grow their hair long or walk down the street with an affected gait. Most of them are married and lead a completely normal family life. When one sees them off the stage, it is difficult to believe in their transformation.

The most highly paid Jatra actor today is Phani Bhushan Motilal, popularly known as Chhota Phani (younger Phani). He earns 3,300 rupees ($695) per month. He started his career at twelve as a chorus dancer, appeared in the role of a singer-dancer, played female heroines, and later specialized in heroic roles. Today, at sixty-two, he still plays the young hero. His most famous roles are Siraj-ud-Daula, the patriotic and last ruler of Bengal who was defeated by the British in 1757; Viswa

The cobbler saint Ruidas meets his long-absent wife Debi, played by actor Hari Gopal Das

(Bhishma), the epic hero of the *Mahabharata* who took a vow to remain celibate throughout his life; and Bharata, the half-brother of Rama who did not accept the throne when his mother had Rama banished for fourteen years. Because Chhota Phani specializes in one type of role—the young, noble hero—many critics do not consider him a great actor, but within his narrow range he has tremendous power. I would prefer seeing a traditional Jatra actor always playing the heroic youth or the old father or the bewitching queen just as I enjoy seeing the Kathakali master Krishna Nayar playing Keechaka, and Raman Kutty playing Hanuman—roles that require specialization and years of discipline. Chhota Phani—a thin, bald, sallow-skinned fellow—takes on height and weight the moment he enters the asar. His voice, his stance, his movements have a stunning appeal. His popularity is tremendous. If he is scheduled and does not appear in the show, even the peace-loving Bengalis may grow violent and resort to brickbatting, or may set the canopied arena on fire. The audience did in fact burn an auditorium in Kakadip Village in 1963 when Phani did not turn up.

Starting life as an orphan, Chhota Phani strode to success. He is known for his money-extracting habits (sometimes he is reported to have charged taxi fare after traveling by bus) and is a terror to the proprietors. He is 100 per cent professional. He takes his breakfast at eleven in the morning, sleeps till seven, and wakes up only two hours before the show. Oblivious to what is happening in the world, he is concerned with his role, his pay, and his audience. Out of spite the proprietors of Jatra troupes call him "the snake" (*phani* means "snake").*

Phani is a popular name in the Jatra world. Apart from the two leading Phanis, Bara and Chhota (Big and Small), there are at least ten more Phanis, all reasonably famous. The one in the Natta Company is Phani Bhattacharya, who plays the Queen Mother in *Petiter Bhagawan*.

Bara Phani Bhushan Bidyabinod, a versatile actor, is at home in many roles. He can play with equal grace the young king, the old saint, the vicious landlord, the sly servant, or the noble father, and because of his versatility some people consider him the greatest Jatra actor.

Some famous Bengali actors started as amateur Jatra players. Among them are Ahindra Chowdhury; the late Chhabi Biswas; the late Teenkauri Mukherjee; Jauhar Ganguli; the late Phani Roy, who alternated between the films and the Jatra;

---

* The name Phani Bhushan actually means "one who wears the snake as an adornment," that is, Shiva.

and the stage and film actor Nitish Mukherjee. An actor who
has once known the challenge, the openness, the vitality of the
Jatra will always long to repeat the experience.

MUSIC

While folk and classical music have distinct personalities,
they come together in the folk theater. There is hardly a good
folk actor-singer who does not know the classical *ragas*. The
prayer song, the mood song, the song of separation are invariably set in classical melodies.

The singing of Jatra had become more and more complex
by the middle of the nineteenth century. In the latter half of
the century, when Bidya Sundar *palas* had degenerated into
mere erotic singing and dancing, Madan Master, a professor
at Hooghly College, introduced the Juri system. *Juri* means
"the double." Madan Master realized that some good actors
were not being used only because they could not sing. To give

An actress playing the princess in a Jatra troupe

a chance to purely dramatic actors he introduced the system of "singing on behalf." He had four singers sit at the four corners of the stage to sing on behalf of the characters, as their doubles. This system he may have borrowed from the contemporary tradition of dance dramas and Raslilas in which the Bhagavatha or the Swami sang the lines of the character. In the modern Western theater, Bertolt Brecht has used this device of singing on behalf of the character in his Epic Theater.

The actor in the Jatra sang the first line of the song and tossed it over to one of the squatting singers, who immediately stood up. The line was then taken up by the singer on the right or diagonally opposite. One after the other the four singers rose in turn as the song progressed. They spun out the melody and added frills and graces, concerned not so much with the words as with subtle elaboration. They released the players and spectators from the burden of literary words and thinned the melody to a fine musical web. Expert classical masters, the Juri singers added interpretative quality to the song.

This suspended the action of the play. The characters on the asar sat down, smoked, chewed pan, and checked their make-up while the four singers continued the melody, passing it from one to the other and carrying forward the musical action like basketball players. Thus the two functions of singing and acting were separated, and the audience could enjoy both in one frame. The Juri singers were also called *mukhtyars*, a legal term of Persian origin meaning attorneys or persons who act on behalf of others. The singers were costumed like attorneys, in narrow clinging pajamas, long black tunics, and big round turbans.

Madan Master also introduced the Dohar system. *Doha* means "the refrain," and the Dohars were people who sang the refrain. Side by side with the Juri classicists, a set of singers simply rendered the refrain, thus helping to bring the etherealized melody down to earth and reinforcing it. The refrain gave the Jatra singing a new strength. The Dohar system was inspired by the Keertan (congregational singing) in which the principal singers sing with musical flourishes and the refrain is taken up by the religious gathering, who beat cymbals and wooden clappers and goad the tempo to a delirious climax.

The musical instruments accompanying the old Jatra were the *pakhawaj* and *dholak* (types of drums), the *behala* (violin),* cymbals, and flutes. As a result of Western influence,

---

* Some orientalists trace the word "violin" to an Indian origin. During the Vedic era the stringed instrument *pinga* was played with a conical

which seeped into the folk theater through the British Raj, clarinet and trumpet were also incorporated. Today these are essential in a Jatra performance.

Nineteenth-century journals often commented upon the musical quality of Jatra performances. *Samachar Darpan* (July 13, 1822), reporting about a new Jatra *Nala Damayanti* ("The Love Story of King Nala and Princess Damayanti"), wrote: "The musical score in various *ragas* and classical melodies was accompanied with dance and dialogue and created atmosphere."

A large repertoire of classical and semiclassical melodies goes into the Jatra. The favorite modes are *bageshri, arana, bhairav,* and *bhairavi.* In plays of historical grandeur or with mythological themes, the classical *ragas* always evoke the period.

Minor characters—servants, gardeners, attendants, robbers, monks—mostly use folk tunes (Bhatiali and Keertan melodies) to depict their work-a-day existence. The first concert at the opening of the play is always set in a classical *ragini.* The second concert is light. The orchestral music follows the mood and character.

THE VIVEK

The Juri system continued till the first decade of the present century. By the second decade people were tired of the Juri because it continued for hours, spinning fine melodic gossamers that suspended the theatrical enjoyment. It had become a sort of an exercise in classical singing out of proportion to the drama. The public would boo and hiss if the singers overdid their long musical performance. Slowly it went into disrepute.

In 1911 Mathur Shah, a shrewd businessman and owner of a company, asked his music director, Bhootnath Das, if he could devise a means of discarding the Juri system without injuring the song element. Bhootnath introduced the Vivek system in the play *Padmini* ("The Self-Immolation of Queen Padmini") by Haripada Chatterjee, which the company was rehearsing at that time.

The Vivek is a character who can appear in any scene—in a bed chamber, in a king's court, in heaven, in hell, in a burning ghat, in a forest, in a street. He enjoys unrestricted freedom.

---

bow. Later the name was changed to *bahuleen,* which meant an instrument played by resting it against the *bahu* (arm), and from this came *behala* (the Bengali word for violin). Another name of the *pinga* was *ravanstra,* as the epic demon king Ravana played a prototype of the *pinga* by resting it on his arm ("The Indian Origin of the Violin," by Dr. V. Raghavan, *Journal of the Music Academy,* Madras, XIX [1948], 65–70).

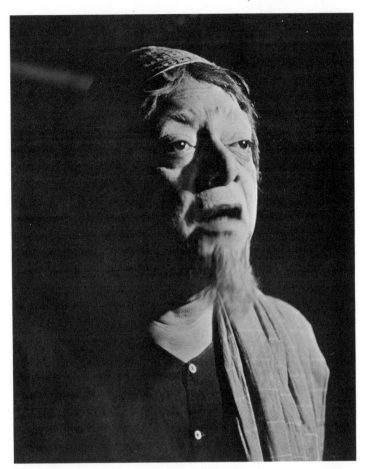

The famous singer Teenkauri Bhattacharya as a loyal Muslim servant (the Vivek) in Bhuler Mashool

Vivek means "conscience." When a character does something wrong, the Vivek turns up to warn him in song. If a king is doing an injustice, the Vivek suddenly appears to check him. Dressed like a madman—his eyes glazed, his head and feet bare, his beard tangled—he wears a robe of black, saffron, or white. His movements are sharp and conclusive. He enters the gangway on the run and disappears in the same way.

The Vivek has a definite dramatic function. He comments on the action by his song, externalizes the feeling of the character, plays his double, and puts questions to him. He is everybody's shadow, a running commentary on actions and events. He lives in the past, present, and future. The role is always played by a highly paid singer.

The Vivek was popularized by Ahi Bhushan Bhattacharya, a playwright-actor. In his mythological drama, *Surath Uddhar* ("The Rescue of King Surath," 1915), the first line of every song was: "Look into your own self and proceed along. This is the proper time!" This line came to represent the period.

The early Vivek had freedom and mobility. Its philosophical transparency was clouded by playwright Brojindra Kumar Dey, who turned it into a concrete character in *Swarna Lanka* ("Golden Ceylon," 1925). In *Swarna Lanka* the Vivek is represented by Bibishana, brother of King Ravana, who advises him to return Sita to Rama and thus avoid war. He is the voice of justice. He sings the conflict in his own mind, philosophizes, and comments, but he does not really impersonate the Conscience.

The playwright can impart the Vivek's qualities only to a noble character who preaches the doctrine of Life. This character could be the brother of a villain, a truthful old servant, a begger, a monk, a guru. In *Banglar Bodhu*, by Nanda Gopal Roy Chowdhury, the mad beggar is the Vivek. In *Bargi Elo Deshe*, the poet Ganga Ram voices the truth. In *Bhuler Mashool*, a popular hit of the Navaranjan Opera Company, the role is entrusted to the Muslim servant of a Hindu landlord. It is played by the famous tragic basso Teenkauri Bhattacharya, whose eyes glow as he sings and evokes the mood.

The development of the Vivek from the abstract to the concrete narrows down the function of the character. He can sing out his own mind, but not the minds of other characters. He does not evoke the other side of the human being with the theatrical reality of the abstract Vivek.

JATRA ON WHEELS

The Jatra has regained popularity during the last five years. There is a growing restlessness and feeling of boredom with the city professional theater. Except for Utpal Dutt's Little Theater Group, which performs permanently in Minerva

Theater, and Sombhu Mitra's Bohurupee Company, which plays fitfully though artistically, the commercial stage is in decay. The realistic tradition has been played out. The Jatra professionals represent a robust acting tradition in Bengal.

In Calcutta there are twenty-one Jatra troupes, ten permanently professional and eleven *thekawali* (actors engaged temporarily on contract). Each offers about three plays a year. They open their season in September and perform nightly until the monsoon breaks in June. All the troupes are then disbanded, and the actors are free to join any company. The manager—the only person on permanent staff—spends the rest of his time clearing the accounts and "abducting" good actors with tempting offers for the coming season. The actors are shuffled like cards and redistributed. Each signs a legal agreement for nine months and is given a pay advance according to his caliber.

The Jatra addicts know that the artistic standard of a company changes with the changes of actors. As in Chinese restaurants in San Francisco, where the master cooks carry the gourmets with them to the new restaurants every time they change their place of work, the Jatra stars carry with them the loyalties of their fans. The Navaranjan Opera was the favorite in 1962; the Janta Opera brightened its glamour in 1963; the Natta Bharati was the chief attraction in 1964 because of Chhota Phani and the comedian, Hiralal Bannerjee. Only the Natta Company, headed by Surya Dutta, maintains a sound artistic standard year after year, and for this Surya Dutta's personal magnetism is responsible. Some of the actors have been with him for thirty years, and this has given the repertory a style and stability.

The Jatra is highly organized. Controlled by private individuals, the troupes work through impresarios called *dalals* —the middlemen—who set up the itinerary. This frees the ensemble from the worry of where it will perform next. Unlike a professional city company, it does not have to bother with the sale of tickets, and the manager does not cast a worried look on empty chairs. There is always a throbbing, colorful mass audience. No microphones or amplifiers are used. In this the Jatra stands distinct from the Nautanki and the Tamasha, which have vulgarized their art by the use of loudspeakers.

The leading Jatra troupes visit the states of Assam, Orissa, Bihar, and distant towns of Bengal. They are invited for festivals, fairs, marriages, and housewarming ceremonies and are paid from one thousand to two thousand rupees per performance, plus lodging. They even perform as far away as Varanasi and Delhi, which have large Bengali populations.

In most district towns, such as Hooghly, Nadia, and Bardwan, Jatra competitions are held during the Durga Puja festival. The chiefs of coalfield areas and tea plantations arrange special shows for their workers and organize contests in which half a dozen Jatra troupes are invited to perform each night in turn. The head of the locality or organization that invites the troupe pays a lump sum. He arranges for the stage, lighting, pandal (improvised auditorium), gatekeepers, living quarters, and open-air kitchen. Here food is cooked by the Jatra troupe which travels with utensils, cooks, and servants. When invited for an occasion such as the laying of the foundation stone for a school or a temple, the troupe accepts a smaller fee. On a commission basis, it charges 60 per cent, and the rest goes to the organizers for the good cause.

A Jatra actor playing a Muslim chief in Bhuler Mashool

The salaried staff of the leading companies varies from forty to sixty individuals, and their pay for a month varies from twelve thousand to fifteen thousand rupees plus food and traveling expenses. A leading actor—a hero, or a villain, or a

Vivek, or a male "actress"—gets between five hundred and two thousand rupees per month, a much larger sum than the respectable professional theater offers.

The Jatra company is a single man's concern. The proprietor puts in the money and engages everybody on contract. To launch a good Jatra troupe (costumes, instruments, advance payments to actors, paraphernalia of conveyance and kitchen), he must spend 35,000 to 40,000 rupees. A humbler company can be started on 20,000 rupees.

Most districts have professional Jatra companies, but these do not command popularity beyond their own locality. There are thousands of amateur Jatra companies. Calcutta alone has hundreds. Each street religiously performs a Jatra with the help of the amateur actors during Durga Puja.

Today a Jatra performance, like a professional city theater, generally starts on time, although the commissioned performances may be delayed by half an hour because of the slovenliness of the organizers. In a village or a small town the touring Jatra group maintains a tight schedule. Sometimes it performs two plays a night.

A Jatra play is written with a technique all its own. The most famous living author is Brojindra Kumar Dey, a headmaster in a small town school. A prolific writer, he has the knack of building climaxes and piling situation upon situation. He does not bother about literary excellence or complex characterization. An efficient craftsman, he draws upon readily acceptable historical and romantic tales.

Political color is especially apparent in the Jatra. Plays on the Partition, Hindu-Muslim unity, patriotism are a big draw. The Bengali political consciousness never fails to express itself in the arts. This quality gives the folk theater a contemporary ring. In the 1930's the actor-director Phani Bhushan Bidyabinod wrote *Neel Kothi*, a play on the life of the indigo plantation workers. It is a sequel to Dinabandhu Mitra's *Neel Darpana* ("Mirror of Indigo Planters," 1865), which portrayed the first phase of the farm laborers' social awakening and created a stir throughout India. The British banned the play. *Neel Kothi* was also suppressed by the British, and the author was confined to his town. Another politically zealous Jatra composer-singer was Mukand Das, who died a few years ago. He was jailed many times for his anti-British *palas*.

A Jatra play is not published if it is on the boards. In the absence of strict copyright rules, a rival company may steal the lines, the songs, the situations. If the printed text is available in the market, the actors feel they are playing a stale drama, a second-hand work; its freshness is lost. The audience misses part of the suspense and thrill.

Actor Sunil Roy as the heroine in Bhuler Mashool *casting amorous glances at her lover*

The introduction of female actresses has shifted the balance in some Jatra companies. They are losing their traditional color and heat. Popular film tunes are also invading the form. Cheap songs and bastardized rhythms are devoured by the Jatra, and these are jarring. Often the orchestra plays full blast. The shrill trumpet and clarinets drown out the actors' voices. The musicians do not wear any particular dress. In their greasy vests and rumpled dhotis they look like petty shopkeepers. The stagehands lounge about and have no theatrical bearing. The lighting is dreadful. If the ancient oil-fed torches were used these would add to the atmosphere, but neon lights and diffused bulbs break the focus.

In spite of these drawbacks, the Jatra is dynamic and shapes the artistic consciousness of every Bengali. It still offers more vigor and enjoyment than the well-publicized professional theaters.

Chapter Three

NAUTANKI

NORTH India has two extremes of folk theater: the secular Nautanki and Naqal, and the religious Ramlila and Raslila.

Nautanki, an operatic drama, is performed in Uttar Pradesh, Punjab, and Rajasthan. The earliest dramas of this form were called *sangeets* (musicals). One such musical, *Shehzadi Nautanki* ("The Story of Princess Nautanki"), became so popular in the nineteenth century that the people started calling the form "Nautanki." According to another theory, Nautanki derives its name from *natak* (play), which became *nataki* and later *nautanki*. Some claim that one hundred years ago the admission fee for such performances was *nau takkas* (nine coins), and that from this the form derived its name.

Nautanki evolved out of ballads and the recitals of bards. The ballad singers, as they unfolded their stories, gesticulated and dramatized the emotions of the various characters. Gradually, in addition to the narrator, other singers were introduced to play the different roles. The stories of saints, robbers, kings, lovers, and knights popular in the folklore have been carried on by Nautanki performers, who in many cases use most of the verses of the original ballads.

Nautanki is performed on a waist-high platform surrounded by the audience. After introductory songs in praise of the guru, the stage, and the deity (Krishna, Shiva, Saraswati, or some other), the Ranga (Stage Manager–Director) sings out a dramatic event of the story and ushers in the characters. Generally the play starts with a king's court, a robber's den, or a queen's palace, providing the occasion for dancing and singing. Suddenly some unusual event occurs, disturbing the colorful scene.

The actors in the traditional Nautanki sit on the stage near the orchestra but are theatrically absent. They smoke, chew pan, and get up when their turn comes. If the play is performed in a village square or in a city street, the balconies, housetops, and platforms become the tiers of a gallery. The princess sits in the upper window of a house. The dauntless hero sings out a love song from below, fixes a ladder, and climbs up to meet her. Natural locations and spatial levels are used to advantage.

The orchestra—harmonium, *sarangi* (multistringed wooden instrument), clarinet, and *nagara* (kettledrum)—is on the stage. The *nagara* is theatrically extremely effective. The player sits on his haunches and strikes it with two sticks. With thumps, thuds, and clatters he punctuates entries and exits and underlines the singing.

After the *bhaint* (invocation song), the Ranga sings a couplet. It is followed by the *chaubola*, a four-line song, each line with twenty-eight beats. The *chaubola* singing is concluded

37

by the *daur*, which has four lines, three with twelve beats and the fourth with twenty-eight. The last line of the *daur* is synchronized with a loud stroke of the *nagara* which clatters with a brilliant ferocity. Sometimes the *nagara* gives only a short clatter, as a rhythmic stitch, after which the other character replies. In a duet, the *nagara* provides punctuating strokes. The character starts his song with a short spiral note and fixes the meaning of the song by clearly pronouncing each word. If the audience is large, the characters sing each line on the four different sides of the stage, thus reaching the remotest listener. The repetition heightens the enjoyment. If the audience is small, the characters repeat the lines twice, walking from one corner to the one diagonally opposite.

In *chaubola* singing, the drummer injects fury into the song. The actor explodes into a dance sequence which the drummer carries further by stepping up the tempo. Drunk with its rhythm, he is like a rider whipping a galloping horse.

Chaubola and *behar-e-tweel* are the favorite song forms. *Behar-e-tweel*, a lengthy metrical composition, is good for narrative singing. The finale is the last half of the concluding line, which is repeated like a refrain. The singer goes on doubling and quadrupling its tempo. This breaks the monotony of the long verse and provides an occasion for dance and superb drumming.

The musical scale changes with the singer. Since the music does not have a harmonic pattern as in Western music, the scale can be shifted without difficulty. For this reason the harmonium has become an indispensable instrument, supplying cues to the actor-singers and guiding the shifting of the scale.

Of the large variety of musical meters used, the most common are the *lavani*, *dadra*, *khayal*, *chaubola*, *behar-e-tweel*, *qawali*, and *doha*. When someone appreciatively offers money to the singer, the Ranga announces the donation in an extemporaneous rhyming couplet, weaving together the name of the patron, his profession, village, and family, and the names of his father and grandfather. The singer accepts the donation with a bow and puts it in the hollow of the *sarangi*.

Men act as women. Since the main expression is through music, the boys acting females do not stress acting nuances as much as singing. Their high-pitched voices must be melodious. When people go to see a Nautanki they do not care who plays the harmonium or the *sarangi* or the clarinet. They are concerned with the principal singers and the *nagara* player.

THEMES

Nautanki, secular to the roots, is a beautiful blend of the

Hindu-Muslim folk cultures. Its language, music, costumes, themes, and characters reflect the mixed social set-up. The austere Muslims who came as conquerors in the eleventh and twelfth centuries slowly adopted the ways of local Hindus, and the Hindus slowly accepted Muslim influence in their arts. During the long Moghul rule, the arts reflected a synthesis of the two cultures. The classical Kathak dancers, steeped in Radha-Krishna lore, are dressed in Persian tunics and girdles. The Rajput miniatures of the sixteenth to the eighteenth centuries are an expression of the gilded refinement of Moghul courts and Hindu myths and legends. The Nautanki also manifests the vitality of the two cultures.

Religious tales digested in the Nautanki have a secular coloring. Even in as sacred a play as *Raja Harishchandra* ("The Truthful King Harishchandra"), when the noble Queen Taramati begs money for the cremation of her dead son, she dances kicking her heels and swinging her hips. In a religious tale Sita sings of her tragic plight while casting "come-hither" glances.

The Nautankis were mostly written in Persianized Urdu with a mixture of Braj, Hindi, and Rajasthani. The courtly language of the Nautankis required the composer to select ornate music and to draw from the classical *ragas*. In actual singing they made the *ragas* more folkish. The chief regional variants of the classical *ragas* are *bhairavi*, *bilawal*, *peelu*, and *khamaj*. The Nautanki singing does not offer musical elaboration. It gives the classical melody a directness, an edge, a rural vigor.

Famous Nautankis are: *Tippu Sultan, Amar Singh Rathaur, Prithviraj Chauhan, Rani Durgawati, Panna Dai*—all historical plays championing valor, honesty, and faithfulness. Among the religious ones are: *Ram Banvas, Shrawan Kumar, Nala Damayanti, Mordhwaj, Raja Harishchandra*. Popular social romances are: *Triya Chritra* ("Witchery of a Woman"), *Reshmi Rumal* ("Silken Handkerchief"), *Shahi Lakarhara* ("The Royal Woodcutter"), *Sultana Daku* ("Sultana, the Woman Bandit"), *Siyah Posh* ("The Man in the Black Mask"), *Sabz Pari Gulfam* ("The Heavenly Nymph and Prince Gulfam").

The story from which Nautanki takes its name tells of Princess Nautanki of Multan, a famous beauty. In a neighboring state live two brothers Bhup Singh and Phool Singh. One day the younger, Phool Singh, handsome, adventurous, and rash, returns from hunting and asks his brother's wife to serve him food quickly. She taunts him, saying that he is behaving as if he were the husband of the beautiful Nautanki. Insulted, he leaves home, vowing that he will not return until he has married Nautanki. His faithful friend Yashwant Singh accom-

panies him. On reaching Multan they meet the flower woman
of the palace and beg her to allow them to stay in her hut.
Every day this flower woman carries a garland of fresh flowers
to the princess. Phool Singh, expert in the art of floral decoration, offers to weave a garland for the princess if his hostess
will cook for him. The flower woman takes the garland to the
princess, who suspects that someone else has prepared it and
flies into a rage. The terrified flower woman explains that her
nephew's young wife has been on a short visit and that she had
prepared the garland. The princess commands her to produce
the young wife and the flower woman returns to her hut greatly
perturbed. Phool Singh calms her, suggesting that he is a superb disguiser and will not be recognized if he puts on a woman's clothes. The flower woman takes Phool Singh, disguised
as a beautiful woman, to the princess, who is struck by his
beauty. She offers her friendship and insists that Phool Singh
stay in her chamber. He agrees. At night the princess sighs
that if Phool Singh were a man she would marry him. Phool
Singh asks her to close her eyes, meditate, and concentrate on
the household deity and invoke her blessings to turn one of
them into a man. This the princess does, and when she opens
her eyes she finds that her friend has turned into a man. A
love scene follows. In the morning the palace maid reports the
matter to the king, who orders the young man arrested and
killed. Nautanki, carrying a sword and a cup of poison, reaches
the spot where Phool Singh is awaiting death. She drives off
the executioners and challenges her father. The king, deeply
touched, agrees to her marriage to Phool Singh.

Nautanki and Phool Singh have entered the vocabulary of
the folk speech. Any beautiful girl dismissing her suitors one
after the other is a Nautanki waiting for her Phool Singh. Hundreds of plays have been written on the theme. Most troupes
have the story of Shehzadi Nautanki in their repertoire.

Siyah Posh is another popular tale. Jamal, daughter of the
Wazir of Syria, is reading the Koran on her palace balcony
when handsome young Gabru passes in the street and points
out mistakes in her recital. Jamal looks at him and invites him
to continue correcting her. He scales the palace wall, and they
fall in love. Every night he meets her in her chamber. One
night, while scaling the wall, he is arrested, and the Wazir orders his execution. Jamal, dressed in a black mask, arrives at
the scene. Her lover is permitted to meet Jamal for the last
time. The king, who has overheard their conversation on one
of his nightly incognito rounds, recognizes the purity of their
love and pardons them. Struck by Jamal's nobility and faithful
love, he adopts her as a daughter and marries her to Gabru,
who is proclaimed heir to the throne.

A Nautanki actor playing the role of a respectable married woman

Raja Harishchandra is the story of an ancient Hindu king who is steadfast in honoring his word. One day Sage Vishwamitra, in order to test him, appears in his court and tricks him into a promise by which he relinquishes his throne, jewels, palace—everything. In the end he is obliged to pay *dakshina*, a fee offered to the Brahmins. Unable to pay, the honor-bound king serves as a slave at a cremation ground. His wife, Queen Taramati, is reduced to working as a domestic servant in the house of a rich man. Their young son is bitten by a snake and dies. Taramati carries the dead child to the cremation ground, but the truthful Harishchandra will not cremate him because she cannot pay the fee. She begs him to chop off her head to save her from further humiliation. He blindfolds his eyes and draws the sword. At this moment Vishwamitra appears, admits the glory of the truthful Harishchandra, revives his son, and restores him to the throne. The story has been celebrated in ballads, plays, musical dramas, and poems all over India. Films have been made on the theme. Every Indian child knows the story and is moved by the scene of Queen Taramati walking in the street with her son's dead body in her arms.

An important nineteenth-century musical drama was *Indrasabha* ("The Court of the God Indra") by Agha Hassan Amanat, the Urdu poet of Lucknow. Amanat used traditional melodies, folk tunes, and seasonal dances, adding to these his dramatic lyric talent. The operatic play went into many editions during his lifetime. Every professional theatrical company during the second half of the nineteenth century staged *Indrasabha*. Various Nautanki troupes modified the original to include their local myths, characters, situations, and melodies. *Indrasabha* stands between literary drama and folk play. Its popularity invigorated·Nautanki writers, who sought to emulate its whimsical and otherworldly atmosphere of fairies, devils, gods, princes, wizards, and dancers.

Nautanki stories are full of noble bandits, brave fighters, and truthful lovers. They emphasize courage, nobility, and gallantry. Events take place at a fast pace. Gods, wizards, and nymphs have free social intercourse with kings, palace maids, robbers, and landlords, creating a fanciful world with intense appeal.

The language is simple, direct, strong. It has no literary density. In the mid-nineteenth century Urdu had already become a definite dramatic language because of court patronage and the tradition of sophisticated poetic symposia. The Nautanki writers cast off the heavily-padded Hindi vocabulary and employed chiefly the more plastic Urdu.

The opening prayer song, *mangalacharana*, is invariably in Sanskritized Hindi because of its religious atmosphere. The rest of the songs and the alliterative dialogue flow in a hybrid form with a heavy Urdu bias. The writers mix Braj, Rajasthani, Hindi, and local dialects in the play, and for this reason Nautanki plays are not generally highly assessed as literary works in spite of their dramatic quality. Their popularity with rural audiences, however, is tremendous. Most villagers are acquainted with the plays, and because of their musical appeal and the directness of their language Nautanki literature sells much better than the best sellers in Hindi or Urdu. People buy basket-loads of this folk literature by weight. A customer may say, "Give me twenty seers of Nautanki." The wholesale dealer weighs cheaply printed plays in a scale and hands them over to retail shopkeepers, who circulate them among the rural folk.

The costumes do not belong to a definite period. King Harishchandra wears the seventeenth-century gilded tunic, while Queen Taramati appears in the contemporary sari. The romantic hero struts in a velvet coat of Western style; the heroine flaunts a sari or a silken *lehnga* (loose flowing skirt).

Women, acted by men, use bright make-up. They apply face powder and mark cheeks and forehead with red dots and silver moons. Lamp soot accents the eyes. Nose rings, earrings, bracelets, and ankle bells add glitter.

Munshiji, the Clown, wears a coat buttoned backward, with a patched multicolored shirt and trousers, and carries a split bamboo in his hand. Munshiji means "accountant of the household." He was a popular character in the nineteenth-century palaces of nawabs and landlords, always appearing at an unfortunate moment to remind the mistress of the accounts. Knowing the seamy side of life, Munshiji moved among cuckolds, disguised lovers, mistresses, and gallant warriors, breaking the serious mood by his financial logic. He appears in Nautanki as an all-knowing man whose incongruous remarks make people laugh. Sometimes he wears a hat or a Turkish cap. He can wear any absurd costume, make any crazy remark, appear at any moment. Whenever the play drags he enters, bringing in a splash of color.

AKHARAS

There are five important *akharas* (schools) of Nautanki: Hathras, Muzaffarnagar, Saharanpur, Kanpur, and Kanauj, each named after the town in which it originated. Of these Hathras and Kanpur stand out for their individual styles. The Hathras was given a robust form by Indarman and perfected by his pupil, Natharam Gaur of Hathras. The Kanpur is led by Srikrishan Pehalwan, an actor-singer-composer-wrestler of Kanpur who owned a Nautanki company. Both these men were exceedingly popular forty years ago.

Natharam started his career as a young boy. He had a melodious voice and danced superbly. He played the heroine, always a beautiful princess or the daughter of a chief. Indarman's troupe became famous because of Natharam. When Indarman grew old, he handed over the company to Natharam, who established a big professional troupe in Hathras. For years Natharam held sway over Uttar Pradesh, earning fame and fortune. His Nautanki, with its densely textured singing, erotic acting, and lusty dancing, became the famous Hathras school. Over sixty plays, including *Raja Harishchandra* and *Siyah Posh*, are ascribed to him, though at least half of these were actually written by Indarman and other people.

The Hathras school has produced many famous actors. Karan, a good singer and dancer-director, appeared on the stage with over two hundred medals pinned to his satin tunic. Actresses were an additional attraction in his troupe. Deep Chand, popularly known as Deepa, was a favorite thirty years ago. His troupe traveled up to Calcutta and Rangoon. Now over eighty, he lives in retirement in a village in the Braj area. Anno and Shyama, two Nautanki dancing girls of Etawah, were tremendously popular in the thirties. They still take part in Nautankis and still have drawing power because of their personalities. They have ringing voices and perform well even today.

The Kanpur school, though it uses the same texts, differs in its style of singing and production. The Hathras lays stress on classical singing and ignores dramatic action. The Kanpur style is simpler, subordinating singing to the needs of the dramatic action. In the Hathras, the invocation is sung by the Ranga, after which he introduces the play. Before the invocation the singer sings a *dhrupad* (a majestic, slow, classical form), always in honor of a god—Shiva, Rama, or Krishna. *Dhrupad* singing demands a highly trained voice, well grounded in the classical art. Not many *dhrupad* singers are left in the Nautanki. The tradition is dying. In the Kanpur style the actors do not sing an invocation but bow to the instruments, offer a Muslim salaam, and squat on the stage. Then follows a *nagma* (a style of song).

Kanpur troupes perform on a picture-frame stage. The drop curtain shows a palace or a garden with the name of the company inscribed on it. Three more curtains represent the jungle, the bazaar, and the court. The players enter and exit from the wings. The audience sits in front. The Kanpur style has changed the folk character of staging and absorbed all the vices of the decadent professional theaters. The Hathras, on the other hand, is open and free, played on a three-foot-high rectangular stage surrounded by spectators. The orchestra sits

A Nautanki actor playing a tantalizing woman of the street

in a semicircle on the stage. The actors move freely on all sides. Boys playing female roles are a big attraction. Before the performance they are kept hidden from public gaze. The eager, toddy-drunk spectators vie with one another in presenting gifts to them, and sometimes feuds erupt. One famous Nautanki "heroine" some thirty years ago was a good-looking boy called Allah-hoo, who had earned this name by singing the *Allah-hoo* song.

Because of its commercial character, Nautanki has attracted women performers. Its secularism has wiped out almost all of the religious elements, and it has become increasingly lewd. In Maharashtra, the Tamasha woman sparkles in the performance; in the north the Nautanki woman is emerging. After the adoption of the Suppression of Immoral Traffic Act in 1959, many prostitutes and *nautch* girls, forced to leave their professions, joined Nautanki troupes. In Kanpur, a Nautanki company consisting solely of female artists makes use of film tunes and other cheap melodies and emphasizes tantalizing gestures in its performances. The city corporation has banned the performance of Nautanki companies within municipal limits. The troupes perform on the outskirts of the city, and the townsmen flock to the gay performances. But it is the old Nautanki troupes with their all-male casts that preserve the vigor, the singing style, and the operatic beauty of the form.

Some folk theatrical forms closely resembling Nautanki are the Bhagat of Agra, the Khyal of Rajasthan, and the Maanch of Madhya Pradesh.

BHAGAT

Bhagat, a four-hundred-year-old form of operatic drama,* was in its earlier stages a dramatized Keertan singing with a thin story. Nautanki owes its birth to this old form and is called its "daughter." The word *bhagat* means "the devotee," and those who performed the drama in the earliest times were devotees of the Vaishnava cult. Later stories of kings, historical romances, and chivalric tales were introduced, but the form never lost its religious character. Today there are Bhagat *akharas* in Mathura, Vrindaban, Agra, and places associated with religious fervor. In Agra in 1827 Ram Prasad of Amroha and Johari Rai of Motikatara produced a legendary folk play, *Roop Basant*, the story of two brothers who suffered at the hands of their stepmother. The *akhara* was founded, and Johari Rai was acclaimed as its first guru.

The Khalifa is the administrator of the troupe, and membership is awarded strictly on his recommendation. The new

* This form of entertainment is mentioned in *Ain-i-Akbari*, the monumental sixteenth-century record of Akbar's court.

member presents a turban to the guru, touches his feet, and offers sweets to be distributed among the members. Only then is he admitted as a disciple of the akhara. Annual contests are held between different akharas, in which only members can take part. Nautanki, on the other hand, has no such restrictions. Any actor can be employed by a Nautanki troupe or invited or loaned at commercial rates. A Bhagat performance, unlike a Nautanki one, is free because of its religious background and social status. Nautanki uses a mixture of Urdu, Persian, Braj, Hindi, and Rajasthani words. Even English phrases appear, and any novelty is welcome. But Bhagat employs only Hindi, Braj, and Urdu vocabulary. In Nautanki women act; in Bhagat only men.

The preparing of the Bhagat stage—a high platform—involves a long ceremony. The guru fixes the first pole; then the construction starts. The stage is dressed with flowers and colored cloths with religious motifs. When the rehearsal starts, all the members gather in the dressing room. The guru, well versed in rituals, plants his handprint in yellow on the clay-coated wall. The script is kept before the handprint, which symbolizes an auspicious beginning. Near the wall a lamp filled with ghee is lighted and a cow-dung cake smolders, emitting fumes that are considered sacred. The nagara clatters, the musical instruments are played, and a bhaint, or prayer, is sung in honor of the goddess—Saraswati, Lakshmi, or Shakti.

The ceremony is repeated on the day the play is to open. The action begins with the entry of Ganesha (or Ganapati), the elephant-headed god. He dances wearing an elephant-head mask, vermilion trousers, and a yellow satin jacket. After his introductory dance, he sits on a chair and the Khalifa offers worship to him. After Ganesha's exit, a bhaint is sung in honor of the goddess, followed by various prayers commemorating famous gurus and personalities. These prayers are generally sung in couplets and chaubolas, followed by the daur, the finale of the musical composition. The Ranga then appears and acquaints the spectators with the story, theme, and action to follow. The performance lasts until the small hours of the morning.

The concluding ceremony is Jyoti Shanti. The actors gather in the dressing room and sing bhaints to the gods and goddesses, thanking them for their "presence" during the performance. The guru puts out the flame of the ghee lamp, ending the ceremony.

KHYAL

The Khyal of Rajasthan is lyrical in temperament. The name probably comes from the Urdu word khyal, meaning "imagination," perhaps because the Khyal is an operatic drama without realistic setting or décor, which depends upon the imagination of the audience. It is also possibly a corruption of the Hindi word khel, meaning "a play."

Its themes are historical romances, love tales, and religious stories full of chivalry. The tradition of heroism for which the sandy land of Rajasthan is famous has been popularized by Amar Singh Rathaur, Balaji, Prithviraj Chauhan, and Tejaji. Ballad singers of this region depict the valor of their chiefs, kings, and local Robin Hoods. The Khyal became a popular dramatic form in the early eighteenth century when Rajput miniature paintings were expressing the heroic life of the land with fine line and color. Romantic plays include Laila Majnu, Pathan Shehzadi, Sultan Nihalde, Dhola Maru; religious ones include Raja Bharathari, Narsi Bhagat, Nala Damayanti, and Draupadi Swayamvara.

Khyal includes a variety of styles derived from famous composers and regions. The Kuchamani style owes its name to Lachhi Ram of Kuchaman, who introduced melodic variety and vigor in the dance steps. The main meters are: doha, lavani, kavit, dubola, and chaubola. He wrote over two dozen Khyals which are performed today by professional groups. The Shekhawati style (from Shekhawati region) was created 150 years ago by two brothers, Jhali Ram and Prahladi Ram, of a rich Brahmin family, who blended the folk melodies with classical ragas and raginis. The principal ones are: jaijaiwanti, asavari, mand, chandravali, sorath, malhar, and des. The Khyal actor-singer does not depend upon rehearsals since the theme and the song are known to everyone and are sung in daily life at parties and fairs.

MAANCH

Maanch is the lyric drama of the Malwa region in Madhya Pradesh. The name Maanch originates from manch, "the stage." A week before the performance, the flagstaff, or stage pole, is fixed in place according to the old Sanskrit tradition, and the guru, generally the playwright-actor, performs the ceremonial worship. The stage is open on all sides. In earlier times it had an extension where the village nobility and officials sat. There was also an arrangement for instrumentalists to sit at another stage level.

The play begins with the entire cast on stage in full costume and make-up, their hands folded and their eyes shut, singing the invocation. The Bhishti (Water Carrier) sprinkles water and sanctifies the stage. The Farrason (Attendant) spreads a carpet. The Bhishti and Farrason act out these services while singing the glory of their functions. Then the Chopdar (Herald) announces the play, introduces the characters, and sets the mood.

Most actors in Maanch are from the artisan classes: goldsmiths, tailors, carpenters, gardeners, coppersmiths. Only men participate. The one exception has been an eccentric woman, Babajan, who appeared in heroic roles and wore a turban and a loose-sleeved shirt. She performed on the Malwa folk stage until twenty years ago, when she died at the age of eighty-four.

The dialogue of the characters always ends with a refrain, sung by the instrumentalists and the actors and punctuated by the *dholak* (the drum). The language is traditionally Malwi, although now Hindi is also being used. Modern Maanch was started by Guru Balmokand, who died while still a youth, during a performance of *Genda Pari* ("The Fairy of the Marigold Flower"). He left sixteen plays which have been printed and are still popular in Malwa.

Chapter Four

BHAVAI

BHAVAI is the folk theater of Gujarat, the homeland of Mahatma Gandhi. Backward, puritanical, inhibited, the people are known for their shrewd business acumen. Big industry in Bombay and most of the cotton mills in Ahmedabad are owned by Gujaratis. The rich and the middle class are colorless. But the farmers, craftsmen, and village artisans, poor and less inhibited, bring color to their folk arts.

The Shakti * cult flourished in Gujarat in the seventh and eighth centuries. Out of nine worship centers of the goddess Kali, three are in Gujarat: Mahakali in Pavagadh, Bahucharaji in North Gujarat, and Amba Mata in Arasur—the three manifestations of the Goddess of Power. In the ninth century Kayavarohan, twenty miles from Baroda, was the center of the Vammarg cult in which sadhus practiced perversions in the temples and indulged in sexual orgies of the most extravagant type.† Followers of this cult believed that the sexual was one of the paths to spiritual enlightenment and that, by exhausting the enjoyment of carnal pleasures, the devotee could make himself free of them. As a reaction, puritanical Jainism and the Vaishnava cult of devotion flourished. King Siddharaj of the Solanki dynasty, which ruled until the thirteenth century, was a firm believer in nonviolence and vegetarianism.

Gujarat state retains the two extremes. The upper classes are prudish and preach nonviolence and puritanism. The lower strata derive energy from the worship of Amba Mata, the Goddess of Power.

The Bhavai is performed during Navratri—nine nights coinciding with the Dashahara festival—in front of the shrine of Amba Mata. The players are convinced that the goddess attends the performance.

The word bhavai has several interpretations. Bhav means "life," bhava means "sentiment," and vahi means "carrier" or "a diary." So bhavai could mean "carrier of life," "expressive of sentiment," or "a diary of life." The actor says: "When I come onto the stage, Shakti, the Goddess of Power, sits on my face, and Saraswati, the Goddess of Learning, on my tongue."

The Bhavai was started in the early fifteenth century by Asaita Thakar, a Brahmin of the Audichya clan (there are eighty-four subcastes of Brahmins in Gujarat). He recited scriptures, singing the texts and explaining their meaning to the devotees in the precincts of a temple in the town of Sidhpur. An unusual incident turned Asaita into the originator of a new form of drama. Ganga, the beautiful daughter of the

* Shakti, meaning "power," also stands for the goddess Kali, who has various manifestations.
† Erotic sandstone sculptures of that period have recently been found in Galteshawara in Gujarat.

farmer-headman of a neighboring village, was abducted by a Muslim chief. The villagers were infuriated, but no one dared challenge the Muslim. Asaita Thakar went to him and pleased him by his singing. In return, he asked him to set Ganga free, claiming that she was his daughter. The chief, knowing that Hindu orthodoxy did not allow a Brahmin to eat from the same plate as a farmer's daughter, put the poet-singer to the test and asked him to eat with Ganga. Asaita ate and thus brought her back, but he was ostracized by his community. This turned him against Brahmins. He left his village with his three sons and decided to earn his living by singing and acting. He composed playlets attacking social injustice, prudery, and the caste system.

The village headman, Ganga's father, was grateful to Asaita and promised that in the future village headmen would look after the needs of Asaita's sons and grandsons wherever they performed. The tradition has continued till today.

Asaita's sons, Ram Lal, Rattan Lal, and Madan Lal, carried on the tradition. The three sons were boycotted by society. Their families were called Trigala, which means "three houses." Today Trigala is itself a caste and the inheritor of Bhavai drama.

Asaita was a learned singer and poet. He left 360 veshas (playlets) of Bhavai of which most are still performed today. Vesha means "dressing up," "masking," or "a scene." A vesha lasts from half an hour to three hours, depending upon the performers. Many people wrote veshas after Asaita, but these are cheap imitations.

For five hundred years Asaita's veshas have been performed by the Bhavai troupes. In every period people added elements of their contemporary life—characters, anecdotes, social oddities, jokes, new trends—and here and there they changed the language. Urdu, Hindi, and Marathi words mix well with Gujarati in the veshas since Gujarat has always had cultural pressures from the Hindi-speaking North and the Marathi-speaking Southwest. But the songs, the staging, and the frame of the Bhavai playlets have remained the same.

Asaita's plays are an integral part of every troupe's repertoire. A famous one is *Joothan Mian* ("Honorable Mr. Brag"), a burlesque in which the hero, a king in disguise, boasts and tells fantastic lies. *Kajora* ("The Ill-matched") is about a fat woman married to a boy. Its sexual references cause riotous laughter. In *Chhail Batau* the hero falls in love with Mohana Rani. Some playlets are pure character studies—a tribesman, a scavenger, a merchant's wife, a sadhu. *Ramdeva*, generally performed as the concluding item, is a chaste drama packed with proverbs and parables.

In one night eight to ten quite unrelated playlets are performed. They are strung together by the Naik (Director), who comments on them and links one playlet with the next. Song, stylized speech, and dances are interwoven. The performance is held in an arena at ground level.

In spite of the deep devotion of the players to the goddess, the Bhavai is secular at its roots. Its jokes, dances, themes, and songs deal with the life of the common people. Mythological heroes are rare. It is the saucy maid, the miserly merchant, the betraying wife, the romantic stranger, the lascivious old man, the braggart, who regale the audiences.

The woman in Gujarat observes purdah, an influence of centuries-old Muslim rule and Hindu orthodoxy. She draws the *ghungat*, an extension of the sari drapery, from her head down to her chin in order to hide her face. Holding one end of the *ghungat* between her thumb and index finger, she draws it across her face and looks through the fine muslin or silk as she talks. She speaks even to her husband from behind the veil. Angry, loving, shouting curses in the street, beating her children, fetching water, blowing at the fire in the hearth, she never lets go of the veil. It is a part of her head. Because of purdah, men always take the part of women in the Bhavai.

THE ARENA

In the dressing room, one hundred feet from the arena, the actors light a big earthen lamp brimming with mustard

oil. It is placed on two bricks near the wall on which Amba Mata's *trishul* (trident) is symbolically drawn with white dots around it. The actors pass their hands over the flame and then over their eyes and foreheads to incorporate light. They dip their fingers in the sacred oil and rub it on their faces before they start making up.

The sputtering lamp is the incarnation of Amba Mata. A symbol of power, it gives light and dispels darkness. The actors worship it. They put incense, fruits, camphor, and coconut in front of it. Scented red powder and white *abil* dust are sprayed as an offering.

After putting on their make-up, the players sing a devotional song, *garbi*, invoking the goddess, and then walk to the arena, where the Naik draws a circle with a ten-foot radius on the ground using the point of his sword. This is the acting area (*paudh* or *chachar*). The spectators squat all around. The actors and instrumentalists, sitting in the *paudh*,

sing five devotional songs. Then they rise and invoke the
Mother. The Naik sings out a couplet: "O Mother come and
bless us!" Two singers repeat the lines. The *paudh* is a sacred
place, and only the performers can enter it.

The instrumentalists are placed on one side. The Pakhawaji
has a drum slung horizontally around his neck. The *narghan*
player has a pair of small drums tied around his waist, and
he plays them standing. One man jangles the *sarangi*, producing the subtlest undertones and overtones. (The harmonium,
a recent vulgarity, has now become very popular in the villages.) The cymbal player adds metallic rhythm and clang.
The most dramatic and unusual instrument is the *bhungal*,
a five-foot-long copper pipe with a tapering mouthpiece and
a large, bell-shaped end. The *bhungal* folds up like a telescope.
Its trumpetlike sound is used effectively for entries, exits, and
climaxes, and to set the tempo. The two *bhungal* players must
have good breath control and stamina.

When the first invocation is sung, only the *bhungal* notes accompany it. No drum or cymbal is allowed. No one dances. Everyone is in meditation so that the Mother can come. During the invocation all the players are in the *paudh*. The actors who are to be in the subsequent scene then quietly disappear. The players slip into the dressing room in turn as their cues approach. Otherwise, they remain in the arena. They sit and join the chorus or relax or help the instrumentalists. Every one of them can sing and dance and play an instrument.

All entries to the *paudh* are by a gangway that runs through the crowded audience. The entry of a general, a king, or a procession is always preceded by guards and servants holding small flaming torches. The Naik, always present in the *paudh*, sings a couplet about the *vesha* that follows. The *bhungal* sounds shrill blares: *dhe-te dhain, dhe-te dhain, dhe-te dhain!* or *dhai-tain dhai-tain dhai-tain taiaiain!* * warning the players to get ready.

After this the god Ganesha is invoked. Elephant-headed Ganesha is worshiped before any other god by devout Hindus —merchants, priests, and actors. There is a folk legend about his birth. The story goes that once Parvati, the wife of the great god Shiva, was bathing in her sunny courtyard. Fearing that somebody might intrude, she made a clay figure, breathed life into it, and placed it to guard the gate. Meanwhile, Shiva returned from the forest. When the young boy guarding the door would not let him in, Shiva was infuriated. He challenged the boy, cut off his head, and walked in. The naked Parvati was surprised to see him. Shiva told her that an arrogant boy had stopped him and that he in anger had killed him. Parvati cried that this was her son and that Shiva must bring him back to life. Shiva ran out and found that the head was gone. Seeing an elephant coming down the road, he chopped off the elephant's head and quickly put it onto the boy's bleeding neck. By his supernatural powers he then brought the boy to life. Parvati wailed to see her grotesque son. As a penance for his hasty act, Shiva granted the boon that in the future the elephant-headed boy, Ganesha, would be worshiped as the first deity.

The actor playing Ganesha wears ankle bells, a yellow silk dhoti, a silk jacket, garlands, and a cap. He holds a shining brass plate and moves it horizontally and vertically before his face, giving partial glimpses of his eyes. The brass plate serves to hide his face since no one is expected to impersonate Ganesha. This method of representing Ganesha is much more

* These are dance and rhythm syllables.

expressive of the dignity which the god should command as the chief deity than is the elephant head with tusks worn by the actor in the Jatra, Therukoothu, and Veedhi-natakam dramas.

When the prayer to Ganesha is over, the village barber walks through the passage carrying a big brass torch. Its mouth is filled with cotton seeds soaked in oil which throw a bright flame. In olden times the torch was invariably of silver if the Bhavai troupe was prosperous. In many temples today silver and gold torches are used when the Bhavai is performed in honor of the Mother.

The barber sits on his haunches at one side in the *paudh* holding up the torch and feeding it constantly with oil from a metal can. When an important character is to strike a pose —a close-up—the barber promptly rushes to him with his flaming torch and moves along with him, highlighting his facial expressions; or he gets up and joins the entourage of a king or a queen or a victorious general, adding pomp to the royal grandeur. He knows his moments. A devotee of the goddess, he sits alert all night. He is the lighting effects man.

The performance starts at about nine in the evening and continues until eleven o'clock the following morning. Most *veshas* last from thirty to forty-five minutes, but important ones, such as *Jhanda Jhoolan*, *Joothan Mian*, and *Chhail Batau*, last for hours.

A sequence of dialogue completing a thought process or an incident is marked by a brisk dance phrase. The Naik speaks out the drum syllables: *tata-thai thai, tata-thai thai, tata-thai thai ta!* The characters—a king, a milkmaid, a merchant, a robber—dance to the rhythmic syllables, which are repeated three times. This breaks the monotony of the spoken word and stitches together the rambling dialogue.

The Ganesha sequence is followed by the character sketch of a Brahmin. Then *Joothan Mian*, a rib-splitting burlesque, is presented. Joothan, a fantastic character created five hundred years ago by Asaita Thakar, is always played by the Rangalo (Clown). He wears a conical turban with colored tassels. His chalky clown's face is dotted with red and black, and he wears bells around his shins. He stomps about, telling bombastic lies. He greets the audience: "To the squatting people I offer a squatting salaam; to the standing spectators, a standing salaam; to the fat ones, a fat salaam; to the slim ones, a slim salaam; to the tall ones, a tall salaam; to the pigmy ones, a pigmy salaam! . . ." He sticks out his red tongue and dances.

He brags and barks and mimics. He imitates a woman, a king, a thief, a wrestler, as he goes on narrating his exploits. A master boaster, he is transparently absurd and naïve. The audience enjoys his lies. He says, "I saw an ocean of milk . . . I can chop off my thumb and fix it again . . . I can swallow a sword." This is the wishful thinking of a man who wants to achieve the impossible. He takes refuge in the most extravagant lies and multiplies them. This releases the audience from the bondage of truth.

Joothan Mian, the bragging Buffoon

Joothan is Muslim and has two Hindu wives, Chatki and Matki. Both nag him and pull his leg, but he never capitulates. He is the gay spirit, the born optimist. He improvises situations, jumps over hurdles, and is always ready for the next adventure.

According to the fable, he is the disguised king of Bokhara, wandering in search of the truth. He had once marched with a big army to invade Ghazni. On the way a camel loaded down with equipment collapsed and died. The king ordered his minister to make the camel stand up and walk; the animal was wasting precious royal time. The minister explained that the camel had died and its soul had departed, leaving behind a carcass. The king asked about the soul and life after death. The minister replied that only a yogi or a spiritual man could explain these things. The king reflected that he too would some day collapse like the camel. He recalled his army, abandoned his throne, and, disguising himself, set out in search of the truth. Arriving in a town in India he began to play the boaster and took upon himself the lies of the whole world in order to purge the people of their falsehood. In the mask of untruth he is seeking the truth.

This sequence is followed by *Kajora*, a skit about a fat wife and her boyish husband. The woman says: "My ill fate, a stripling is my husband! My parents ruined my youth by marrying me to a lad. I want to swallow poison. When I go to his bed he turns his face away and snores. When I clasp his hand he whines. I am large and big. I can lift him in my lap and rock him in my arms. To whom shall I tell my woeful tale?" And she narrates her troubles.

This scene reflects the social conditions five hundred years ago when Asaita wrote. Even today most marriages are arranged. The boy and the girl have their first encounter in the nuptial bed. *Kajora* exposes social inequities, sexual morbidities, family quarrels. It is a biting satire on life and a highly entertaining theatrical piece.

Around midnight, when the audience has had its fill of laughter, *Chhail Batau*, a serious play of social injustice and love, is usually performed. The Naik leads the play by putting questions to the hero, who reveals his identity, his origin, and the whereabouts of his beloved. He is Batau, come in search of his love, Mohana Rani. The Naik narrates the story of chivalry, battle, elopement, and betrayal while it is acted out by the characters, who sing, dance, and improvise, expressing themselves in duets. The tale is full of action, dance songs, and events and is in great demand by audiences.

In *Poorbia*, a woman betel-seller* defies her husband and goes away with her lover Poorbia, the Stranger from the East. He carries her shoes in the bundle on his head. The Rangalo (Clown) taunts him:

Rangalo: Why are you carrying the shoes of a woman? In

---

* The betel-selling woman is considered a common flirt. It is an art to fix a betel leaf with a layer of juicy red katha, a dash of white slaked lime, small pieces of areca nut, sweet-smelling cardamoms, and spiced herbs. Delicately folded, covered by a silver tissue leaf, it is pinned with a clove. The courtesans of Banaras and Lucknow in the nineteenth century perfected the ceremony of betel-leaf offering to their patrons and made it a ritual of high-class manners. The betel-seller keeps a number of spiced juicy leaves inside her jaw and is constantly chewing and throwing smiles to her customers, who indulge in amorous jokes with her. If she is old, her stall is a center of scandal and sex gossip.

Gujarat not even a henpecked husband would think of performing such a low act!

Poorbia: Does a man never help his wife in your land?

Rangalo: In my land a man worth his mustache never helps a woman. But . . . if a woman has her monthly period and her husband washes her blood-stained skirt, this is permissible!

According to social standards of manhood this is the lowest act in a farmer's house. The Rangalo mockingly refers to it. Henpecked husbands who boast of their manly pride in village squares are exposed in such *veshas*.

Another important Bhavai is *Jhanda Jhoolan*, written by Moti Ram Naik early in this century. In this play the wife of a miserly Hindu merchant falls in love with a handsome Muslim youth. The husband arouses the village against the young Muslim, and the wife follows her husband. The Muslim lover becomes a fakir.

When it starts graying in the east, a few sharply etched character *veshas* are performed. These are slices of life, interesting studies. Some popular ones are *Mian-Beewi* ("Husband-

The Rangalo (Clown) and his wife

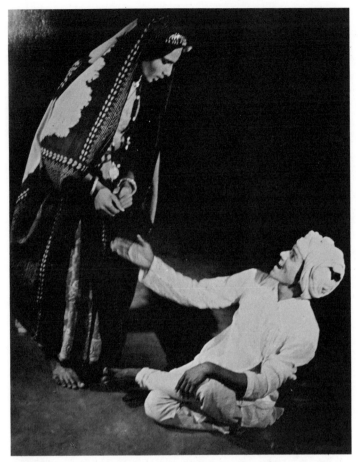

A villager orders his wife to bring food for him (Bhavai vesha)

Wife"), *Pathan* ("Tribesman"), *Marwaran* ("The Woman of Marwar"), *Bawa* ("The Monk"), *Dhed* ("The Scavenger"). The quick changes of roles in these sketches are a test of the chameleon actor's art.

This boisterous hilarity early in the morning alerts the dosing audience and prepares it for *Ramdeva*, a chaste play of literary excellence. In it, Asaita describes the instrumentalists, the players, the spectators, their positions, and the ritual. It begins: "Here sit the drummers in a pleasant mood, here the audience to clap, here the *bhungal* men to blow, and near them stands the Rangalo. Asaita says that now *Ramdeva* will be staged. People have gathered at the shrine of Amba Mata. The immortal flame burns brightly. Many renowned people have danced and sung here. I am the dust of their feet. Let the spectators sit in peace! He who listens with feeling, Amba Mata will fulfill his wishes. The connoisseurs are here. Let ignorance and stupidity vanish! If I speak less or speak too much, O Amba Mata, do not be angry with me!" The Naik sings a devotional song in praise of the goddess.

The Rangalo as a rich moneylender

The main characters of the play are King Ramdeva, his queen, and the Rangalo. The queen challenges the wisdom of the king and competes with him in parables and riddles. The Rangalo translates their words to each other, repeats what they say, replies on their behalf, puzzles them, and acts as their double.

The Rangalo enumerates various types of weights and

measures, planets, seasons, medicines, sweetmeats, names of kings, clans, and family trees of the village people, dazzling the public with his memory. He speaks the verses in a hurried singsong fashion, keeping the significant details clear. The last half of each line is repreated for emphasis. This form of recital was popular in olden times with bards who sang of the glory of heroes.

At the end of this *vesha* a prayer is sung. The two actors playing the queen and Ganesha walk rhythmically in a circle in the *paudh*. The *bhungal* blares, the drums roar. The actors walk to the dressing room with stylized steps. All the players follow. They sing a devotional song, take off their ankle bells, and the performance concludes. The sacred flame is always present in the dressing room. The actors remove the lamp from its place, and this means that the goddess Amba no longer resides in the flame.

A Bhavai troupe generally consists of fourteen people: the Naik, who is the director, stage manager, and leader of the party, and who holds a license to perform in different villages; the male actors (Veshgor and Veshacharya) playing the hero and the secondary hero; the actors of the female roles (Kanchaliyas) of heroine and secondary heroine; the clown (Rangalo); and the instrumentalists. The troupe members are expected to observe celibacy for six months during performing time in order to preserve their power. Wrestlers also do not go near a woman for months before their bouts. Hindus generally believe that celibacy contributes to will power and physical energy.

While women are rapidly taking their place in the Nautanki and Jatra folk theaters, and the Tamasha of Maharashtra already has female dancers as the star attraction, the Bhavai, though in a crumbling state, is strictly guarding the traditional ban on females. The best Bhavai actors specialize in female roles. Some men known throughout Gujarat for female impersonations are Jayashankar Bhojak Sundari, Moolchand Vallabh, Lalubhai Chokri, and Pransukhmani Lal Naik.

THE FEMALE CHARACTER

Every important female character enters through the passageway holding two lighted *kakras*. The *kakra* is a cloth soaked in oil and tightly rolled so that when lighted at one end it burns like a torch. She brandishes the *kakras*, weaving fire circles as she walks rhythmically down to the *paudh*. She is dressed in a billowy skirt, a spangled blouse, and a colorful *orhni*, a short sari draping the head and tucked up at the waist into the skirt. She is called Kanchaliya because she wears a *kanchali* (blouse).

Bhavai actor dressed as the Kanchaliya, the female dancer

Standing in the center of the *paudh*, the Kanchaliya dancer holds the lighted *kakra* between the thumb and index finger of each hand, points the flames toward the ground, and jerks them. The overflow of the sizzling oil is thereby cleared. Then, crossing and weaving the *kakras* in the air, she places her wrists on her temples with the torches flaming overhead and looks at the audience. This means that she is blessing them. She sweeps the torches to the left, folds her hands, joins her palms with fingers apart, and makes a salutation. Then she waves the torches toward the right and salutes with the same ritual. This is an offering to the goddesses of the two directions.

She traces a circle with quick steps, goes to the instrumentalists and the Naik, and kneels or sits on her haunches. Touching her ankles with her palms, she bends her head low, rolls her eyes, and receives the blessings of Saraswati (the Goddess of Learning) and of her guru, the Naik.

Then she stands up and sings without dancing. The words of the first line are expressed with facial gestures. After the audience has grasped the meaning of the opening line, she proceeds to the next one and dances, occasionally bringing the torches near her face to show a particular emotion.

The dance is counterclockwise, the left hand always facing the center of the *paudh*, and the right the surrounding audience. The drum syllables are: *dhinna trikit tinna trikit*. The drummer produces these rhythmic syllables, and the dancer beats them out with her feet as she circles. The tempo is doubled. The *bhungal* joins in with shrill gasps, reinforcing the tempo. The beat takes the form of this sound pattern: *ghe-ghe traka-dhinna, ghe-ghe traka-tunna....*

The dancer sits down and places the torches on the ground. They are picked up by the barber, who blows them out.

The *orhni* drape gives a beautiful frame to the dancer's face. The various styles of holding it reveal anger, love, disgust, abandon, happiness, defiance, or shyness. Holding both the ends of her fluttering veil in her right hand, the dancer moves rhythmically, casting glances to the right and to the left so that all the people can see her face as she flashes past them. This hiding and revealing is typical of a Gujarati woman's shy coquetry. When the tempo quickens, the dancer holds the ends of the veil in her left hand and, partially lifting it, moves with speed, keeping her right hand on her hip. She sparkles in her half-lifted veil—an expression of excited defiance.

In Gujarat a respectable woman must keep her head fully covered. But, if she is a mistress or an abducted woman or a prostitute, she can let her *orhni* slip down and reveal her bare head. In order to show that she is addressing her lover, and not her husband, she drops the *orhni*. Interweaving her fingers and placing her clasped hands behind her head she yawns, casts glances from the corners of her eyes, and walks proudly displaying the glamour of her bosom. This is an open invitation to clandestine love.

In a group dance the women take a step forward, then backward, then forward, bending alternate knees after each step. They move in a circle, swinging their hips as they sway and bend and stream forward. In their colorful orhnis, they make a superb colored, geometric pattern. At the conclusion of the dance they whirl and jump and end by sitting on their haunches with their skirts spread around them.

Bhavai singers are high-pitched. The words of the songs are clearly pronounced, the meanings vividly portrayed. They use classical ragas, devotional hymns, and folksongs. The classical melodies most used are: des, sorath, sarang, sohani, poorbi, prabhat, ramkali, bilaval, kalingra, asavari; the folk and devotional singing includes these forms: bhajan, garba, ras, doha, ghazal.

MAKE-UP AND COSTUME

Each actor carries his own costume and does his own make-up. The colors most used in make-up are white, red, and black.

The characters of humbler social status—a washerman, a farmer, a barber, a merchant, a scavenger, or a gardener—do not use make-up or period costumes. For instance, in a play about a Moghul emperor, characters such as the boatman and the police constable would be wearing present-day attire.

Kings and chiefs have exaggerated mustaches and eyebrows and a faint reddish paint over their faces. A king's costume is a mixture of the Moghul and the local Gujarati folk style. The tunic is tight at the waist and flares below. The pajamas are narrow at the calves and bulge at the thighs. A golden cone shoots up from the middle of the turban.

The Brahmin is dressed in a thin, red-bordered white dhoti. The sacred thread (janiyau) runs from over his left shoulder across his bare chest down to his waist at the right. On his forehead are three lines of sandalwood paste with two crimson spots in the center. Wearing a tilted cap on his close-shaven head, he carries a brass jug in his hand and scriptures under his arm.

The most picturesque make-up is that of the braggart Joothan Mian. A chalk-white stripe runs up his nose and branches into three, one arching around each eyebrow and one extending to the crown. Black and red dots decorate his cheeks. He wears a silk turban wrapped around a golden skull-cap with tassels, a glittering tunic, baggy trousers, a sword, and a shield.

In the eighteenth and nineteenth centuries when the Bhavai was at its peak and actors won high posts and rewards for their art, they wore gold-laced tunics, gold-embroidered blouses, and silver-spangled skirts. The orhni was threaded with gold. Today the costumes are still colorful, but no longer of real gold and silver.

Skirts are full and billowy. Twenty-six yards of cloth go into the making of a skirt with flares and flounces, heavy for a city maiden to carry. When the woman dances, the skirt spins and whirlpools. If the character is a merchant's wife, her skirt is thicker and brighter. A shepherdess from Kathiawar is dressed in a black *jimmy*—a saronglike dhoti.

The actors have very few costume changes. The same actor may be many different characters. By tilting his turban and changing his gait, a smart young man becomes a fat money-lender. By changing the position of his shoulder scarf he is transformed from a cringing astrologer into a proud pundit. He tucks up his dhoti and he is the village headman or the stupid weaver. The same dance steps with a little variety in facial expression can suggest a majestic king, a limping beggar, or a waddling shopkeeper. This is the art of the actor. An old Bhavai actor said to me: "My guru did not use any make-up. He chanted the name of Amba Mata, dipped his palms in the lamp oil, rubbed it on his face, assumed a new look. Modern make-up is not a good thing. An actor should change his face by inner juices. My guru transformed himself into a villain or a noble hero by control of his facial muscles."

The Bhavai emphasizes character acting. Some of the characters immortalized by the performing troupes are Joothan Mian, Chhail Batau, Jhanda Jhoolan, Chatki and Matki (two saucy wives), the Marwaran (Woman from Marwar), Teja Sethani (the bewitching wife of a miserly foolish merchant).

The Bhavai, like the Tamasha, is down to earth. Women do not go to see it, and this allows the players more freedom in vulgar jokes, abuses, and off-color remarks. In the printed text, references to corrupt officials and abuses do not appear because of the censor. The publishers use dashes or leave blanks, which the actor fills in with an abusive rhyme or the name of a popularly hated official.

Very few mythological playlets appear in the repertoire. Apart from *Ganapati* ("Worship of the God Ganesha"), which is the prologue to every performance, these are the known ones: *Ardhanarishwara*, which presents the god Shiva and his consort in one unified body, half of which is male and half female; *Rama Lakshmana*; *Taraka* (the ogress in the *Ramayana*); *Kahn Gopi* ("Krishna and a Milkmaid"); and *Bahucharaji* ("Goddess of Power"). Famous historical plays are: *Jasma Odan*, *Shuro Rathaur*, *Ramdeva*, and *Jai Singh*. None of these playlets is as popular as the social satires.

The Bhavai is an inherited art. The Trigala community, descendants of Asaita Thakar who originated the form in the

fifteenth century, is the chief preserver of its dramatic
beauty. The people are farmers, generally from North Gujarat, who take to Bhavai as a part-time profession. For six
months—from mid-September to mid-March—their troupes
tour the rural area. They are socially bold. If a Hindu girl
abducted by a Muslim is recovered, the orthodox Hindu
family will not accept her, but the Trigalas will receive her
because of their ancestor's fight for social justice. Because of
their unorthodox way of life they were considered low, and
the scholarly Brahmins would not accept their writing as
literature. The high-class poets shunned them. That is why
Asaita's writing, unique in its humor and literary pungency,
still stands as the chief source of the Bhavai performances.

Turis and Bhils, two communities that practice Bhavai in
humbler surroundings, are uninhibited. The Bhils, of tribal
origin, use their own dialect. They eat meat, drink wine, and
add coarse speech and wild dancing to their performances.

The Nagars, well-placed Brahmins, are followers of Amba
Mata. Every year they perform at the shrine of the goddess at
Pavagarh. Those who cannot go to the shrine perform as a
ritual before the image of the Mata in a temple or in a courtyard. They do not collect money. With them it is pure ceremony, an offering to the Mother. During the Navratri festival,
they grow barley shoots in earthen pots. The barley symbolizes
fertility. The healthier the growth of green shoots, the better
life will be in the coming year. On the tenth day, when
Ravana is killed by Rama, they pluck the green spikes, tuck
them in their turbans as they sit worshiping the Mother, and
throw the pots into a pond or a river. The women of the
community sing and dance the Garba for nine nights in the
streets and courtyards and offer their worship.

The following castes also perform the Bhavai as amateurs:
the Vahivanchas (keepers and readers of family chronicles);
the Kansaras (coppersmiths); the Kachhiyas (vegetable-
sellers); barbers; tailors (who do not use vulgar speech because
it is believed that if they do their needles will stitch their
tongues); Ghanchis (oil sellers); Koli (low-caste farm laborers); and Vaghari (reapers of corn and water-carriers).

A thick mixture of Hindu and Muslim cultures prevails
in Bhavai social plays. Muslims, against whom there has al-
way been a religious bias among respectable Hindu families
(who will not drink from a Muslim pitcher), are gallant heroes
in the veshas. Even when a Muslim character abducts a
Hindu woman, he is painted not as a villain, but as a charming
man of dignity. The target of ridicule is the miserly Hindu
trader.

In the seventeenth and eighteenth centuries the Bhavai

actors received gifts from local chieftains and rajahs and were given good posts in their courts. Many troupes performed in the presence of mighty Peshwas in Poona and were awarded gold *janiyaus* (sacred threads worn by Brahmins across their chests). Since the plays were filled with contemporary comments and biting remarks on life, especially on corrupt officials, the Muslim rulers discouraged the performances. The reformist movement during the latter half of the nineteenth century shattered the already crumbling form. The purists waged war against its vulgarity, the naked jokes, the unashamed references to sex, and the constant appearance of a flirting wife whose husband, the merchant, was often shown as not only a cuckold, but impotent as well.

The middle class was rising. By the close of the nineteenth century the business class was a definite force in urban life. When the Gujarati professional theater, modeled on the Western three-act proscenium style, was established, most Bhavai actors joined. No women came forth to act the realistic heroines in the new plays, and the Bhavai actors filled the gap with their "feminine" grace. The great actors of the first quarter of the present century came from the Bhavai-trained families.

The new stage was more respectable, and there was more money in it. Educated people were its patrons. The illiterate Bhavai actors rose in social status and received recognition in these companies.

Amrit Keshav Naik, an all-around performer, was the first known Bhavai actor to join a professional company. Moolchand Vallabh (playing the saucy Chatki) rose to the position of the director of the Laxmikant Natak Samaj Company. The equally famous Jayashankar Bhojak Sundari started his career at the age of thirteen as the beautiful heroine, Sundari. Later on he became famous under his feminine name. Now over seventy, he is still a force in the Gujarati theater. Vithal Das Bhojak, Moolji Khushal Naik, Pransukh Naik (who appeared in silent films as Eddie Polo), Lalubhai Chokri, and Pransukhmani Lal Naik (the last two specialists in female roles) were Bhavai actors.

Some actors who did not leave the Bhavai and continued to dominate the arena are Motiram Naik (writer and director-actor of *Jhanda Jhoolan*), Shamlal Vallabh Naik (who played the gallant Chhail Batau), and Durlabh Ram Poria Naik (brilliant as the bewitching Teja).

Among today's better Bhavai actors are Vithal Das Tribhovandas Naik, who plays the Kanchaliya female roles; Vishnuram Naik of Unnava (Batau); and Shankarlal Bombom (Joothan Mian). Amritlal Jeevaram Naik Pansarwala, forty-three-year-old father of four sons and two daughters, is an expert Kanchaliya. His female roles of Teja and Poorban are famous achievements.

Comparing the classical theater with the folk, Amritlal Pansarwala once remarked: "There is no relation between the two. That one is for the classes, this one is for the masses. We travel in the same train. The classical troupe travels in an air-conditioned coach. No dust, no heat, no cold. Pure. Exclusive. We travel in the third-class bogie full of noise, curses, squeals, shouts, sweat. Two different compartments."

Among the contemporary theater workers, Dina Gandhi, an emotional actress, has been responsible for introducing the Bhavai element into modern plays. She first was impressed by folk performances during her work in the left-wing movement in the People's Theater in 1945. She wrote *Lok Bhavai* ("People's Folk Play"), a satire on Bombay life, and, since she was an actress, she introduced the imaginary character Rangali—the wife of Rangalo—and played it herself. The play, a two-hour song-dance-dialogue drama, describes a husband and a wife who come from a village to Bombay, meet different characters—a bus conductor, a moneylender, a hoarder, students (portrayed in different *veshas* strung together)—and are disillusioned. The success of this play showed new possibilities for the form.

In 1954 Rasiklal Parikh, a Gujarati scholar, wrote *Meena Gurjari*, the story of an abducted milkmaid. Dina Gandhi and the old-timer Sundari directed it jointly and staged it for Nat Mandal in Ahmedabad. Its chief appeal was the folk color borrowed from the Bhavai. There were innovations, however. Instead of the worship of Ganesha, the worship of Rangadevata (God of the Stage) and of the *jarjara* (the god Indra's flagstaff) was introduced. Sutradhara and Nati of the Sanskrit tradition appeared in the beginning. The dance steps and rhythm were predominantly of the Bhavai, especially in the climactic scene of abduction when Badshah and Meena converse in song. Dina Gandhi played the milkmaid. She made dramatic use of the *orhni*, copying the traditional Bhavai Kanchaliya who masterfully casts glances from behind the veil. The play had an unprecedented success and soon became the symbol of new theater.

Chandravadan Mehta, a popular satirist, wrote *Ho Holika* (1956), which describes a crazy judge who smokes opium, barks orders, and makes wrong decisions. The Rangalo and Rangali, in the Bhavai style, comment and carry the action further. The Song and Drama Division of the Government of India performed *Aram Raj*, a hilarious propaganda comedy modeled on the Bhavai. The village chief sits on a hammock-

Meena Gurjari, the milkmaid, taking leave of the village headman as she peers out from her palanquin

like bed and is carried by his assistants to different locales. He constantly smokes a long-stemmed hookah, holds the rod of justice (a split bamboo stick), and cackles. His decisions are absurdly comic, yet amazingly correct. The opium-eating judge in *Ho Holika* and the clownish chief in *Aram Raj* have a medieval flavor.

The folk theater of Gujarat is slowly making itself felt in the cities. But the Bhavai players today are living in more deplorable conditions than ever. They are not strongly organized, nor are they as sought after as the Jatra players of Bengal or the Tamasha singers of Maharashtra. In the areas of Kutch and Kathiawar in West Gujarat, more than two hundred Bhavai troupes roam the villages. Their art has been so damaged by the popular films that they have mostly discarded their traditional dancing and singing and adopted current film tunes.

During the nine nights preceding Dashahara, however, they still perform the traditional *veshas* in the service of the goddess Amba. They consider this a social and artistic debt to the Mother which they must pay every year.

Chapter Five

TAMASHA

THE AUSTERE Moghul emperor Aurangzeb spent the last eighteen years of his life (1689–1707) quelling the rebel chiefs of South India and the Western Ghats. The sturdiest resistance was from Shivaji, who led the expert guerilla warriors, the Marathas. The imperial army, camped in the valleys and hills away from home, hungered for entertainment. Singing girls and dancers were imported from North India to amuse the bored soldiers.

The Dombari and Kolhati, acrobats and tumblers of the local communities, learned the northern dance style readily and joined the entertainers. The local poets composed songs in Marathi. The traditional Gondhalis, who sang and danced in praise of the goddess Parvati, influenced the newly developing form of entertainment, the Tamasha. *Tamasha* is a Persian word which traveled to Maharashtra and Deccan through the Moghul armies. It means "fun, play, entertainment."

The Gondhal singers used the *tuntuna* (a one-stringed instrument) and *manjeera* (a pair of small metal cymbals). When the Tamasha form was evolving, these two instruments were incorporated in it. The *tuntuna* and *manjeera* players sing the refrain. When the main singer stops, they take up the last line. Their voices jump to an astoundingly high pitch. The old ballad form of Powada, which the bards sang describing the heroic deeds of a king or a chivalric knight, contributed to the vigor of the Tamasha. In the Powada narrative singing today, the traditional *tuntuna* and *manjeera* players are the refrain singers.

When Aurangzeb died in 1707, the power in Maharashtra passed directly to Shahu, Shivaji's grandson, who established his throne in Satara, the citadel of Maratha power. He had eight ministers. The prime minister was called the Peshwa.

Because the ruler was weak, the Peshwas became powerful enough to shape the history of the Maratha kingdom. Bajirao I (ruled 1720–40), builder of the Maratha empire, was a great warrior and hunter, and fond of dancing. Chhatrasal, the rajah of Bundelkhand, was pleased with Bajirao's heroic deeds and presented him with a beautiful dancing girl, Mastani, who, riding on horseback, went to wars by the side of Bajirao and became his consort. Singers, poets, and Tamasha dancers thrived during his rule. In his personal diary, Shahu mentions gifts of land and jewelry to Tamasha players.

For one hundred years the Tamasha flourished in the Maharashtrian land. Bajirao II (ruled 1796–1818) had classical singers, musicians, and dancers in his court. He was musically wise and politically foolish. His indulgence in the arts resulted in his losing his kingdom to the British. When

73

he was dethroned and sent to a small town in North India, he was allowed to take with him his singers, musicians, and dancers.

Because of its erotic elements, Tamasha was in general spurned by the upper class. The first people to join in this form of entertainment were Mahars and Mangs, two outcast communities. The Mahars, scavengers by hereditary profession, had joined the army as fighting men. Shivaji had a Mahar platoon. Even the British continued the tradition.

The dark-skinned Mahars form the backbone of Tamasha. Their women have a swarthy sleekness. In Poona one sees them sweeping the roads and at once recognizes them by their sturdy grace. They consider themselves socially higher than the Mangs and other untouchables and take pride in the fact that the late Dr. Ambedkar (cabinet minister and framer of the Indian constitution) belonged to their community.

Tamasha was at its height during the late eighteenth and early nineteenth centuries. In spite of its low social status and lewd associations, it attracted many high-caste Brahmins. The greatest Tamasha composers of the latter half of the eighteenth century were Anant Fandi, Ram Joshi, and Prabhakar, three noble Brahmins who were disowned by their community.

The most famous of these three was Ram Joshi (1762–1812) of Sholapur. His elder brother turned him out of the house because of his association with Tamasha dancers. Ram Joshi went to Pandharpur where in the temple of Vithoba, Krishna's manifestation, he learned Sanskrit and philosophy from the priests and returned home. In spite of his religious education, he was still rejected by his family. He again turned to Tamasha people, forming his own troupe and playing in the villages. A superb poet, he composed unforgettable *lavanis*, sensuous poems unsurpassed even today. A courtesan, Bayabai, liked his songs and sang them in her *baithak* (drawing room) to entertain her patrons. She fell in love with Ram Joshi and started living with him. She put his poems to music and sang them in the house, though never openly in the arena.

Ram Joshi earned a lot of money by his performances and lived like a chief. His bullock cart had a velvet hood and embroidered silk curtains, and the bullocks wore golden coats. He left behind passion-charged *lavanis* which are still sung and are the soul of the Tamasha repertoire. He used euphemism, metaphor, and erotic symbols in his poems, which have a high place in Marathi literature. In one poem he uses the word *payodhar* as a pun (*paya* means both "water" and "milk"). The line reads, "Dark clouds full of water," but in the context of the song it means, "Dark breasts full of milk."

One composer of the early nineteenth century was Honaji,

a milkman, who wrote excellent songs that were sung by his colleague, Bala, a tailor. The team was famous as Honaji Bala Gummat. A second great composer of the period was Sagan Bhau, a Muslim weapon sharpener. Honaji and Bala were rivals of Sagan Bhau in the court of Bajirao II, and all were well treated.

During the Peshwa rule, boys acted women's roles. They were called *nachya poryas* (dancing lads). The Tamasha was so erotic that prostitutes and courtesans learned the melodies and dance movements from the boys to entertain their customers.

After the British occupation, the Maratha court patronage was over. In the nineteenth century landlords and their dissolute sons, with no awareness of art or music, became the patrons of Tamasha. In their courtyards Tamasha became vulgar.

One famous singer-poet was Patthe Bapu Rao (1868–1941), a high-caste Brahmin. He was a superb composer, whose fame spread throughout Maharashtra. Although married, he fell in love with Pawala, a beautiful, olive-skinned young girl from the Mahar community. Patthe taught her singing, dancing and acting. Together they formed a troupe that delighted the Maharashtrian public for twenty years. Patthe was ostracized by his community and deserted by his wife and children.

From 1900 to 1920 Patthe Bapu and Pawala were the biggest stars. During those days, Tamasha was performed in Bombay five days a week in three theaters, the Elphinstone, the Bombay, and the Ripon. Pawala was a big draw. Because of her glamour, rich patrons incited her against her teacher-lover Patthe by offering her tempting terms. In 1920 one patron won her away from Patthe Bapu Rao. Broken-hearted, he left the profession and died in penury.

Patthe Bapu Rao was the last of the famous composers. He ushered the Tamasha into the twentieth century. Pawala, the first important woman actress in the Tamasha, established the tradition of women in female roles.

Today there are eight hundred full-fledged Tamasha troupes. Forty thousand people (actors, dancers, instrumentalists, and their families) make their living in this way. Three thousand women actresses on tour perform in the village squares. Most of them come from Pawala's community.

THE PLAY BEGINS

The stage is a low platform, surrounded on three sides by spectators. In cities a regular proscenium stage is used. The Arya Bhushan Theater on Laxmi Road in Poona offers a Tamasha performance every night.

In the village square the play opens with two drummers, the Dholkiwala and the Halgiwala, who are present throughout the performance. The Dholkiwala has a long, horizontal drum slung around his neck. The center of the right face of the drum is crusted with a hard black substance that gives a dry metallic sound. It is tuned to the singer's voice. The left face is covered with a taut skin of plain leather. The player, leaning forward, balances the drum on one outstretched knee, the other foot slanting behind. This characteristic stance makes the player look as if he were constantly ready to spring.

The *halgi* is a small drum made of a wooden hoop with the skin of a goat's belly tightly stretched over one side and the other open. The elastic tissues of the guts weave through the steel rings bordering the hoop. The player heats the instrument over a fire and tightens the skin further. He keeps it at chin level, gripping it in his left hand. The right hand thrums and slaps while the left hand, holding a short curved cane stick in two fingers, pounds with a piercing clatter. The *halgi* is used to quicken the tempo and give a spurt of ferocity. Its clattering din, a harsh *karh-karh-karh*, can be heard on a still night at a distance of three miles. It announces that the Tamasha has started.

The two players slap their instruments with a competitive gusto, each trying to surpass the other.

The drum has a big repertoire of rhythms and beats. It clatters and rumbles and howls. The Halgiwala and the Dholkiwala distribute a sound sentence and play it between themselves, carrying on a rhythm conversation. One chirps out a phrase, the other adds to it a craftily constructed rhythm pattern and throws it back as a challenge. The purpose of this rivalry is not to outwit each other but to build atmosphere and tension.

Two more instrumentalists join the drummers: the Manjeerawala, who plays on tiny metallic cymbals; and the Tuntunawala, who twangs a one-stringed wooden instrument. Gripping it in his right hand, he plucks the string with the long nail of his index finger. The sound, *tui tui tui*, acts as a drone and a beat. These two instrumentalists are the accompanying singers, the refrain keepers. When the principal singer stops for a breath or has sung out a portion of the song, these instrumentalists jump forward and sing loudly in high-pitched raucous voices, the refrain fading out with the sound of *ji-ji-ji-ji*. They reinforce the line, in a high soprano that few female singers could reach. The *tuntuna* player, his right knee forward, his left hand on his ear, twangs his instrument. The *manjeera* player strikes sharp metallic notes, swaying and rocking as he throws his voice from the pit of his stomach. Blood rushes to the faces of these singers. The higher the pitch the more skillful they are considered. Their voices become sharp as needles and fade into piercing whispers. Their twisted faces and eyes look as if they were weeping.

The instrumentalists stand behind the main singer, who performs between the actions of the play to link them up, commenting or carrying forward the story. Sometimes he sings for the character. He is the main singer, the Sutradhara, the leader of the troupe.

The drummers wear a white knee-length tunic, an embroidered waistcoat, a red *shela* (girdle), a *pheta* (turban), and bellows-shaped dhoti tucked up at the back. The dhoti is swathed up around their knees to allow their legs to move freely as they play and spin about. The Halgiwala and Tuntunawala wear almost the same dress with slight variations. If they are prosperous, they wear a silken turban of orange, yellow, or pink with a gold border. In Kolhapur, the heart of Maharashtrian orthodoxy, the Tamasha musicians wear a twenty-five-yard-long turban tilted up from the right and slanting low on the left. Favorite colors are saffron, pale blue, red, parrot green, and magenta. This style is also popular with wrestlers of the area, and the musicians take pride in their heroic turbans.

The drumming is followed by an invocation, the worship of the god Ganesha.

The musicians stand with their backs toward the audience

and move upstage and down singing the invocation. This ceremony, called *avahan* (invoking the gods), is popularly known as *gana*, an abbreviation of Ganesha. Sometimes Shiva and Parvati are also praised in the song because they are the parents of Ganesha.

No woman is present on the stage when the *gana* is being sung. The Buffoon (called Songadya) is allowed to join the invocatory song. At this moment he is serious and dignified.

The next preliminary is the appearance of Gaulan, the milkmaid in Krishna's legend, played by a Tamasha woman. In a classical Sanskrit play the leading actress, Nati, appears in the beginning and converses with the Sutradhara. The Gaulan serves the same purpose. She enters with rhythmic steps and does an erotic dance, hiding her face with the end length of her sari though her head is uncovered. She tantalizes the principal singer and the instrumentalists, who move in quick steps round and round the stage. They talk with the Songadya, the Buffoon, who impersonates Krishna. Krishna is accompanied by his friend Paindia, a deformed, club-footed, quarrelsome cretin.

The incident, taken from Krishna's life, has sexual symbolism and strikes the nonreligious note of the Tamasha. The familiar pattern of dialogue is as follows:

Drummer: Oh, friend, where are we going now?

Krishna (*walking fast in a circle*): To Mathura.

Drummer: What work have you there?

Krishna: Not in Mathura, I have some business on the way.

Drummer: I see! You are going to sell milk and meet the maids.

Krishna: What a wise fool you are! My hands are empty. How could I sell milk?

Drummer: Why are you hurrying, friend? You are walking fast. What's the job?

Krishna: My job is . . . don't you know? My job . . . to tease the milkmaids and drink their milk.

Manjeera Player: From the pots they carry on their heads or from . . . ?

Krishna: I pull at their saris and waylay them. Only then will they yield . . . milk.

Tuntuna Player: Arrr! There she is!

All: Where?

Tuntuna Player (*walks like a woman*): Here she comes jingling her bells and swaying her hips. Listen to the music of her footsteps!

(*The Tamasha woman enters casting glances from behind her sari.*)

Paindia (*holding the Gaulan*): Pay the toll to Krishna. Your milk!

(*She takes down the imaginary pitcher from her head, tilts it, pours milk into Krishna's cupped hands, and sings.*)

After this follows the philosophical interlude of the Sawal-Jawab kee Lavani ("Song of Question-Answer"), a sudden change from the nonserious to the serious to give weight to the program. This item, also called Jhagra (quarrel), is a war of wits between Lord Shiva and his spouse Parvati, or between some other divine pair.

Before the Vag (the main play) starts, a hilarious farce (Rang Bazi) humors the audience. It has *lavani* songs with much improvised dialogue. Most companies perform the following farce. Three friends conspire to visit a woman's house at a time when her husband is away. The woman senses the trick. One of the men knocks at the door. The woman, pouting and simpering, stands three feet away from the anxious caller and gives saucy replies:

Man: Is anybody in?
Woman: No.
Man: Then you are alone in the house?
Woman: No.
Man: Is your husband in?
Woman: No.
Man: Has he gone out?
Woman: No.
Man: May I come in?
Woman: No.
Man: Your husband is not in the house?
Woman: No.
Man (*slyly*): Do you mind if I make love to you?
Woman: No.

He bursts open the door, and the audience howls with joy.

The negative answer of a woman, according to popular interpretation, means affirmation. The villager believes that when a woman says "no" she means "yes," and this is manifested in social ceremonies and etiquette. When a husband tries to lift his wife's veil on their wedding night she is expected to deny him constantly. If she is offered food in her new home (and she is terribly hungry), it is good manners for her to refuse it. The dogged insistence of the suitor ultimately breaks down the door of the negative.

The above preliminaries are followed by the Vag. The themes vary. They deal with chiefs and kings, a merchant and his mistress, a warrior meeting a young maiden in a foreign land, two brothers quarreling over a piece of land, a henpecked husband with two wives. Fairy tales have allegories and flowery symbols. Mythological and historical romances abound. Like all folk plays, the Vag concludes with the moral that truth will shine and falsehood will perish. The hilarious jokes, erotic *lavanis*, provocative dances, and powerful singing and drumming fill the main body of the play.

In the eighteenth and nineteenth centuries the *lavanis* were specially composed and well rehearsed. The dialogue was left to the inventive faculty of the actors. They were given the main points of the story and constructed the dialogue on the spot. They constantly improved and added to the text, injecting freshness at every performance. There was surprise, ready wit, shock. The singer wound up the dialogue by singing the *lavani* and carried forward the story. The *lavanis* lit up the high points, and gaps were filled by the actors with dialogue always leading to the next situation. The actors were clever improvisers, with keen dramatic sense. Nowadays the Vag is written like a play, with dialogue and songs, and the actors no longer need to create their own lines.

THE LAVANI

The *lavani* is a narrative poetical composition expressing vigor and love. It is the spine of the play. The principal singer offers the first line with lusty joy. He starts generally from a high note and goes up the scale. The lines that follow are spoken quickly in a singsong fashion, giving details that make the story move. The singer etches out the meaning of the words with vivid gestures. At a clever dramatic line the drummer thumps the drum and the Tuntunawala and Manjeerawala repeat the line in shrill chorus, summing up the purport of the preceding lines. Their voices are high as they shout in duet. Their wide-open mouths reveal their tongues reddened by betel juice. They have fantastic stamina and breath. The lines fade off into a delirious groan of *hai-hai-hai hay-hay-hay* ... *ji-ji-ji-ji* ..., and suddenly they stop.

For example, if the *lavani* is describing the story of a traitorous general, the song announces the place, the time, and the noble king who has horses, elephants, and a large army. The last line may contain the surprise when the singer adds: "But he has a corrupt general!" These words become the refrain. All of them sing the line, "But he has ...," over and over to reinforce the thematic point.

The singer sings a quick, short aria, a spiral voice flourish, and proceeds to the next line.

The first *lavani* introduces the characters, unfolds the plot, and prepares the audience for the complications. It is followed by bits of prose dialogues again broken by a *lavani*. The song comes at a time when it is expected, at an appropriate moment. Sometimes a dance is introduced to heighten the emotion.

The Tamasha woman punctuates her singing by a burst of dancing. The drummers and accompanists constantly move back and forth in rhythm to impart impulse to the visual scene.

On an average there are thirty *lavanis* in a play, and these take up more than half of the six-hour performance. The *lavani* is of many kinds. The Vag Lavani tells a tale. The Bale-Ghati is a sad song of separation. The Chhakkad Lavani is amorous and colorful; the Dhauti has a fast tempo. The Junnar runs almost on one note, describing the adventures of a country maiden.

The *lavani* is sung with passion. In the "Legend of the Stranger," an old *lavani*, the words have sensual imagery:

> We came to enjoy your body,
> Your breasts,
> And we decided to win the two round fortresses.
> Don't tantalize us;
> We shall enjoy your body forthwith.

The choice of words is always clever and sensuous. North Indian vocabulary and the Marathi language mix well in it because of their earlier association. The classical modes commonly used are: *kalingra, bhairav, peelu, yaman,* and *bhairavi* because these are pleasant and hauntingly evocative.

THE TAMASHA WOMAN

When Pawala of the Mahar caste was accepted by Patthe Bapu Rao of Brahmin background as his spouse, she became

a star heroine. Her image inspired Mahar women, and hundreds of them joined the Tamasha troupes. Kolhati women, acrobats and tumblers, followed suit. During the last fifty years the woman dancer has become an essential element in the Tamasha. Today over three thousand professional women are in the *gummats* (Tamasha troupes). They inherit a vocabulary of lewd gestures from the teen-aged boys of the nineteenth century.

A Tamasha woman

The Tamasha woman wears a bright colored nine-yard *paithani** (silk sari) with golden flowers and border, draped in such a way that the two legs are separated in bellows fashion. A pleated length in front is folded, swept between the loins, and tucked up at the back, leaving the legs free for dance movement. The tucked-up end, a glittering fall, is visible at the back. It makes an effective design and emphasizes the hips. The dancer's green or magenta blouse has smaller floral dots than those of the sari, and the short sleeves have a gold border. Her fingers are ornamented with gold rings and her arms with maroon or green bangles decked with glass bits to lend a cheap sexy effect. She wears a *vazartik* (necklace), *jhubas* (earrings), a shining nose ring, a gold-fringed girdle, and ankle bells.

Her lamp-blacked eyes sparkle and clearly mirror her expression. A tiny red moon embellishes her forehead. The parting of her hair is filled with vermilion powder; the palms of her

* The word *paithani* is borrowed from the town of Paithan, near the Ellora Caves, which is famous for its weavers.

hands and the soles of her feet are dyed pink. Her hair is rolled into a bun because her long braid would disturb the dance movement. She fixes garlands of *shevanti* and *aboli* blossoms around her bun.

She stands in a posture of abandon and relaxation, her body muscles held in tone. Her left hand is placed on her hip with the fingers curled outside; her right arm rhythmically swings back and forth as she walks. In her exuberance she looks like a wild mare. At times she holds the end of her sari and walks in a drunken rhythm, now hiding her face, now revealing it.

The Tamasha dance does not owe its origin to any classical form and is not similar to any folk dancing. While the North Indian Kathak dancer explodes and jumps, the Tamasha woman never leaves the ground, her feet are always near the floor. The heels give the principal beat. Her movements are

Tamasha women wear nine-yard saris, ankle bells, and nose rings, and carry themselves seductively

supple, liquid, exciting. The dance form is a mixture of various elements: the nautch style of North India, the virile grace of the Kolhati acrobatic women, the folk dancing of the area, and above all the impulse of the erotic.

The Tamasha woman is the life and soul of the performance. She bends and sways "like a rice shoot," as the common saying goes. Popularly she is called Nautchi, the nautch girl. Spectators always ask: "Who is the Nautchi?"

Most Tamasha women are unmarried, except for those who play straight dramatic roles. The dancer lives freely with the drummer or the hero or the villain—anyone she chooses—and may bear many illegitimate children. Often quarrels, jealousies, and fights erupt. A dark slim woman, Bhima, in the Nagu Bhagu troupe, said: "We are like Hollywood actresses. We live with the man we like until we are tired of him."

One reason that vulgarity crept into Tamasha is that, until Pawala joined the Tamasha, boys acted as girls and portrayed intimate scenes of eroticism that could not be shown with a mixed cast. The absence of women spectators also gave license to the performers. Today, in spite of the new laws of prohibition and banning vulgarity, the audience reeks with liquor and sex. The very fact that the Tamasha woman is an outcast gives her freedom. She is not one of the audience. She is outside the pale of social morality, and the audience has pushed her to it. Everyone thinks her vulgar and low. She must hit back and be the image they have made of her, show how really vulgar she can be. She shocks the most outspoken rascal in the audience by her remarks. She is the free spirit, a dressed-up nude who brings to light the gestures and words lurking in the heated subconscious of the repressed onlooker.

THE FUNCTIONING OF TAMASHA

The troupes are divided in two types: Dholaki Bari (dominated by drumming) and Sangeet Bari (dominated by music). The Sangeet Bari consists of six or seven people, including singing girls. A harmonium player, a clarinet player, and a drummer sit on one side of the stage. The troupe does not perform a play but entertains with dance-embellished songs. A number of Sangeet Baris may perform one after the other to make a complete program, or they may act as curtain raisers preceding the play. The main Tamasha troupe is the Dholaki Bari, consisting of fifteen to twenty-five players who perform the Vag accompanied by wild drumming.

There are about two hundred theaters all over Maharashtra, with four Tamasha companies attached to each. In the Jalgaon, Kolhapur, and Sholapur areas many professional theaters are run solely for the Tamasha troupes.

In Poona, the heart of Maratha tradition, the only professional house is the Arya Bhushan Theater on Laxmi Road,
which offers a Tamasha performance every night. The main
entrance is a small door decorated with cheap colored lights
and crudely painted posters of dancing girls. An open passage
leads to the yard, which houses many players permanently attached to the theater accommodating about seven hundred
people. The troupes (gummats) work in rotation; some of
them are always on tour. If the visiting company is famous,
the auditorium may be jammed with as many as two thousand
people.

Among the habitués of the theater is a sixty-year-old pleas-
ant-looking man wearing smoked glasses who sits on a wooden
chair in the booking office. His stick rests by his side as he
talks enthusiastically. This is the blind S. G. Gore, a former
tennis champion, the patron of Tamasha. He greets the visitor
with a milky smile. He was my guide at many Tamasha performances. Once he traveled with me many miles in a car at
night on bumpy country roads to Jejuri village to be on time
for a performance. Sitting in the crowd of spectators, he in-
terpreted the songs and the double meaning of the dialogue,
telling me the position of the characters on stage, the names
of actors and actresses, and their background. Though he could
see nothing, he seemed to listen to them "visually."

Daily expenses of the Arya Bhushan Theater are roughly
350 rupees ($74.00) covering rent, the municipal license fee,
electricity, and payment to the staff and the artists. The reve-
nue on lean nights is hardly fifty rupees. The owner of the
theater, Ahmed Seth Fakir Mohammed Tambe, manages four
troupes. The touring troupes make up for losses at Poona.
Ahmed Seth is involved in the business because of the "spice
of life" it gives him. He manages to pay his staff and artists
regularly. If he delays their payment by one night, he says,
"they fly at my throat." He has to maintain a standard, a tradition. He himself lives in a small kholi (lodging), paying eight
rupees per month as rent.

During the six-hour performance every night the spectators
drift in and out of the Arya Theater as their favorite players
come and go. When a saucy Tamasha woman appears, a wave
of enthusiasm sweeps the auditorium. The more chivalrous
types offer gifts and urge her to sing their favorite lavanis. The
government has banned the acceptance of gifts during a performance, but the regular wages in the theater are so low that
nobody objects to infractions. Sometimes an admirer gives
money more for a Tamasha woman's looks than for her art.
She accepts the money, and it is deposited with the leader of
the troupe or the drummer. In the Sangeet Bari, the coins are

kept with the harmonium master. The wings are crowded with instrumentalists. Backstage the Tamasha women sit on wooden benches smoking and chewing betel leaves waiting their turn.

The wage of a dancer in a *gummat* ranges from five to ten rupees. On tour she is given an allowance plus free food. The extra girl is paid two rupees per performance. But around Jalgaon the dancing girls, expert in singing *lavanis*, get fifty rupees or more per night.

The best-known troupe is the Bhau Bapu Khude Narayangaonkar Gummat founded by the late Bhau Mang, who came from the Mang community. He was the disciple and inheritor of the tradition set by Patthe Bapu Rao during the first quarter of the present century. Today his three daughters, Vitha, Kesar, and Manorama, are the female stars, and his nephew, Bapuras Khude (so far the only Sangeet Natak Akademi Award winner of Tamasha), is the leader of the troupe. Vitha, a slim, indestructible dancer, is the mother of six children, and amazingly young and attractive. She jumps and does acrobatic feats, curving her body like a wheel, and dazzles the spectators with her modernized rhythms. Spoiled by success, she has taken to dancing of a hybrid nature. In sober moments she plays the traditional Tamasha woman, but these are rare. The artistic redemption of the troupe lies in the aging Bapuras Khude and the two refrain singers, who inject color and passion into the performance.

Out of many good drummers, Thakkoo, a short, ebony-faced man of fifty-five in Damaji Koregaonkar's company, is in a class by himself. His knee stretched and his head thrown back, he furiously slaps the drum, producing intricate rhythm patterns. His puckered dark hands have tremendous power. Drunk with the rhythm, he pounds the drum and becomes one with it. His eyes spin, and his half-opened mouth dribbles with surcharged enjoyment. One sees only Thakkoo and forgets the presence of singers and actors.

The newly formed troupes have attracted girls untrained in the Tamasha tradition. One such company is owned by two sisters, Lata and Lanka, both exquisitely seductive. Dressed in cheap imitations of the classical Bharata Natyam dance style, they sing film songs and hybrid sexy tunes which they call "modern" form. Gallant admirers pelt the stage with coins. Sometimes one comes up to the stage and places money in the palm of his favorite with a lascivious cluck. The sums offered during a performance sometimes exceed two hundred rupees, three times the fee of the troupe for a performance.

With the introduction of film music and *qawalis* (ecstatic singing), small Sangeet Baris are growing more popular. But it is the Dholaki Baris, with their powerful refrain singers and

drummers and the attractive Tamasha women, which have
kept alive the heroic tales, romances, myths, and legends of
the Maharashtrian people. Their *lavanis* have become a part
of the common man's life.

Thakkoo plays on the drum as a Tamasha woman dances

Dozens of films on Tamasha have been made in Marathi,
most of them successful. The Rajkamal Film Company of
Bombay produced a popular hit on the life of Ram Joshi, the
eighteenth-century Tamasha composer. Recently *Sangate
Aaika* ("Listen to What I Say") ran for two years in one
cinema house in Poona. It tells of a corrupt landlord who
seduces a Tamasha woman and then throws her out. She is
ultimately avenged by their daughter, who also becomes a
Tamasha woman.

Contemporary playwrights have exploited the Tamasha
form in their works. Venkatesh Madgulkar has used the *gana*
(invocation song), the Gaulan (milkmaid), and the Vag
(main play) in *Hutashani* ("The Fire of Holi"). Two head-

men fight over the right to light the fire at the Holi festival. The daughter of one and the son of the other are secretly in love and help to resolve their families' quarrel. The actor-playwright P. L. Deshpande, who gives two-hour solo performances of his own satirical comedies, used the Tamasha in *Sarvodya* ("Good to All"), a political satire. G. D. Madgulkar, the *lavani* poet, is a favorite of amateur groups. Vasant Bapat has many successful modern Tamashas to his credit.

The Tamasha has been a strong propaganda weapon. Active in the Leftist Movement for over twenty-five years, Anna Bhau Sathe from the Mang community wrote political satires using the Tamasha. His colleague, Amar Sheikh, who has a thundering voice, has thrilled huge gatherings of workers with his *lavani* singing. The government cultural troupes have used the Tamasha for propagating the Five-Year-Plan and new projects among rural audiences.

The social playwrights are substituting "clean" humor for the lewd language of the Tamasha. The satirists are replacing sexy humor with political sting. Social reformers are striving to improve the Tamasha moral code by removing its vulgarity. Driven by bigotry they are taking the very guts out of the Tamasha.

What is vulgar for the middle class is not vulgar for the commoner. Sexual references tabooed in the upper class are part of the vocabulary of the village men and women as they fight and curse in the streets. Vegetable sellers, fruit vendors, farmers, cobblers, and fisherwomen use this language with imaginative flavor. The Tamasha caters to this class.

The government has passed a law banning vulgarity in the Tamasha. The emphasis of the Tamasha Board of Maharashtra is on purity of humor. The Vags and *lavanis* are screened, and a certificate stamped "no objection" is required for every performance. The law is limited because the Tamasha is performed in the villages where the policeman comes from the same rural area and understands the place of the lewd jokes. The players improvise, adding double meanings and erotic clowning. The dancer establishes a direct relation with the audience by her coquetry and acts the "public woman" while the spectators whistle and shout and ask her to sing their favorite pieces.

The Tamasha is a theater of release. Its ready wit, free-flowing extroversion, and uninhibited sexual references make the people forget their caste and class.

Chapter Six

RAMLILA

IN SEPTEMBER and October during the Dashahara festival the *Ramayana* story is enacted all over North India in the form of the Ramlila, a cycle of plays based on Rama's life.

The village Brahmin sits in the square at night singing out the epic tale, explaining and commenting on it. The priest blows his conch and chants snatches of the *Ramayana* in the courtyard of the temple. Actors dress as Shiva or Hanuman or Surpanakha (Ravana's sister) and roam the streets at night. Tableaux, song-dramas, pageants, and arena plays in different forms range from bullock-cart floats to modern ballets. This dramatic festival is attended by everyone, from the President of the Republic to a village cobbler.

The events in the *Ramayana* are believed to have taken place about four thousand years ago. King Dasaratha of Ayodhya has three wives who bear him four sons: Rama, Bharata, Lakshmana, and Shatrughna. Rama, the eldest, is married to Sita, the beautiful daughter of Janaka. The aging King Dasaratha decides to relinquish the throne to the crown prince. The second queen, Kaikeyi, interferes. She once helped the king in battle, and in return he has promised to grant her two wishes at any time. Kaikeyi demands that Rama be banished for fourteen years and that her own son, Bharata, be crowned. The king, bound by his promise, is heartbroken. The dutiful son Rama, in order to honor the word of his father, has himself banished for fourteen years. His wife, Sita, and his younger brother, Lakshmana, accompany him.

The king, unable to bear his separation from Rama, dies. Bharata, Rama's loving brother, refuses to accept the throne but appoints himself its guardian until Rama's return.

During the last year of their banishment, while Rama, Sita, and Lakshmana are living happily in a forest hut, Surpanakha, the charming sister of the demon-king Ravana of Lanka, passes their way and tries to flirt with the two brothers. Lakshmana flies into a rage and chops off her nose. She goes wailing to her brother. In order to avenge his sister's honor, Ravana disguises himself as a mendicant and, in the absence of Rama and Lakshmana, abducts Sita. On the way to his golden castle he is challenged by the bird Jatayu. Ravana fatally injures him and goes on. When Rama and Lakshmana return to the hut and find Sita gone, they set out in search of her. The dying Jatayu tells them of the abduction. While the two brothers roam the forests, they happen to meet Hanuman, the Monkey General, and Sugriva, the Monkey King, who promise help. Rama wages war against Ravana, sets his golden castle on fire, and kills Ravana, his brother, and his sons. He finds Sita and returns victorious to Ayodhya. Good triumphs over evil.

The most colorful presentation of Ramlila is in Varanasi

91

(popularly called Banaras, in ancient times Kashi). Two streams, the Varana on the north and the Asi on the south, flow past the city, giving it its name, and empty into the Ganges.

Varanasi has been the center of Hindu thought and culture for over three thousand years. The bard Valmiki, in telling of the *Ramayana*, mentions Kashi (Varanasi) as the glorious abode of Shiva. Religious philosophers in every age had to debate with the pundits of Kashi and defeat them before they could establish their pan-Indian supremacy. Lord Buddha gave his first sermon in Sarnath, a suburb of Varanasi; Sankara-charya, the Hindu philosopher (ninth century); the Vaishnava saint Gyaneshwar of Maharashtra (fourteenth century); and Guru Nanak, the founder of Sikhism (fifteenth century)— all came to Kashi to demolish the tradition-bound superstitions of the local ecclesiasts. Thousands of temples dot the city. Time and again conquerors have destroyed them, but they always rise again. The presiding deity of Kashi is Vishwanath (meaning Shiva, Lord of the Universe), the boon giver, who bestowed boons on both Rama and Ravana, the Good and the Evil. The town offers a spectacle of dramatic contrasts.

Through the narrow Kachauri Lane, famous for sizzling *halwa* and hot *puris*, dead bodies are carried to the Manikarnika Ghat, the famous burning pyre. In this curved lane two fat men cannot pass one another without rubbing navels. The dead are constantly being brought in from neighboring villages and distant towns. The body is carried on a bamboo stretcher by two men—instead of four, as is the death right of every Hindu—shouting to the wayfarers to clear the path. The shop-keepers are busy selling hot *jalebis* and *puris*, and the pilgrims are busy eating them. A sharper contrast of life and death cannot be witnessed anywhere.

Varanasi is famous for its brocades, *ganga-jamuni* (copper-brass metalwork), betel leaves, Kathak dance, *thumri* singing,

and the sacred ghats peopled with pilgrims and close-shaven priests. Every devout Hindu yearns to spend the last days of his life here and die by the banks of the Ganges. Rich landlords, rajahs, and wealthy seths have permanent villas by the bank of the holy river which they keep for occasional pilgrimages and the final exit from life. Decaying, shriveled men; sickly, coughing women; fat priests; long-bearded sadhus; and devout pilgrims throng the ghats. In the midst of this humanity, the temple bells chime, the cymbals clang, and the *Ramayana* is narrated and sung by Brahmins sitting cross-legged in their ritualistic make-up, wearing sandalwood-paste tilakas and sacred threads.

Here four hundred festivals are celebrated every year. There is a saying: "Strange are the ways of Kashi. It holds nine festivals in seven days."

There are the Holi rejoicings marked with bacchanalian abandon in March, the Ved Vyas Fair during the entire month of July, the three-day Rathayatra, the sixteen-day Lakshmiji Fair, and the thirty-day Dashahara celebrations. All are occasions for songs, masks, pageants, street dancing, and carnivals.

Every street in Varanasi has a Ramlila committee. At night, in October, a crowd sits on both sides of the road about every half mile, watching the Ramlila. The road is the acting area. Mythical characters in gilded crowns and masks dominate the rectangular arena with platforms on both ends. On one side is Ravana, on the other is Rama; on one side Evil resides, on the other, Truth. The war of justice is fought in the middle. A half dozen people with tiny cymbals in their hands sit in a circle chanting snatches from Tulsidas' *Ramacharitmanas*, the epic poem on Rama's life.

During his lifetime Tulsidas (died 1624) used to listen to the chanting of Valmiki's *Ramayana* in Sanskrit during the

Navratri festival. Inspired by it, he wrote a massive poem in Hindi about Rama's life. The Varanasi pundits, shocked to see Rama's worship conducted in the tongue of the common man, boycotted Tulsidas, but this only helped to make his epic poem more popular. Through the centuries it has become an integral part of Varanasi life. Seventy per cent of the names of people in the Varanasi area are derived from the *Ramayana*. Among the names are Ram Chand, Ram Lal, Ram Lakhan, Ram Dhan, Bharat Ram, Sri Ram, Sita Ram, all common among high-class Brahmins as well as among merchants and scavengers. "Rama" is added to most names. When a devout Hindu dies, the last word on his lips is supposed to be "Rama." Mahatma Gandhi's last two words after he was assassinated were "Hai Rama." Men and women have their arms and legs tattooed with the figures of Rama, Sita, and Hanuman. Painters, writers, actors, singers, and woodcarvers have drawn richly from Rama's life story. (Recently a marble temple costing six million rupees was built by Seth Thakardas Sarika of Calcutta with the complete *Ramacharitmanas* inscribed on its walls.)

Two years after Tulsidas' death, his devoted follower Megha Bhagat, a dealer in bows and arrows, enacted Ramlila on the basis of *Ramacharitmanas* on the occasion of Phalguni Panch-Kroshi Prakarma. The Prakarma used to last for five days, during which the pilgrims toured the outskirts of the city visiting holy places and shrines. The tradition of Ramlila spread to other parts of the area. Slowly it grew from a five-day pageant play into a festival that may last as long as thirty-one days.

In Ramnagar the pageant of Ramlila is enacted in thirty days. In other Varanasi localities it begins on different dates and its duration varies from fifteen to thirty-one days. The same scenes are not enacted in every locality at the same time. At one place Sita is being abducted; at another Jatayu is engaged in mortal combat with Ravana in order to rescue Sita. Ravana is being killed in one square, while at another Hanuman is flying to the Golden Lanka (Ceylon) with Rama's message to Sita. This avoids repetition.

The performing troupe does not enact all the scenes in the same arena every night. If the action moves from a palace to a jungle, from Ayodhya to Janakapuri, from an ascetic's hut to Ravana's golden castle, the acting area changes. Different scenes are enacted at different places, and these places are associated with the actual locales of *Ramayana*, which are known by their mythological names: Ayodhya, Chitrakut, Lanka, and so forth.

In Ramlila the arena has several settings, each a different

A group of people singing the Rama story in a Varanasi street during the Dashahara festival

acting area at a different level. In one street performance of the Angada-Ravana Samvad scene, Ravana sat on a high pedestal, his throne. At ground level a strip of land ran to the opposite side where Rama, Lakshmana, and Sugriva sat on a platform. A gangway at right angles to the main strip formed an L-shaped level ground stage with bamboo railings along the edges. On one side of the gangway was a circular low stool on which Angada stood arguing with Ravana. The chorus sat at another level, and Sita sat in view in Ashok Vatika as a prisoner in a different place. These multiple stages were islands amidst the sea of people. Voices, chanting, and dialogue came from different locales, offering a magnificent vision—easy, intimate, and many-dimensioned.

The Ramayanis (those who sing *Ramayana* verses in chorus) are an integral part of a Ramlila performance. They sit monkey-fashion on their haunches in a circle, with a yellow-leaved *Ramayana*, illuminated by oil torches, spread

on a mat before them. The light throws an amber sheen on
their faces as they sing in high-pitched voices. They hold tiny
bronze cymbals which produce metallic, caterwauling music
and act as rhythm and drone. When the characters speak, the
Ramayanis are silent. They sing out what the actors say in
local speech. After every quatrain, they add a rhythmic "hay-
haaa," which serves as a carry-forward note to the next. When
the drama requires the description of a scene or the inner
thoughts of a character or a philosophical comment, they
chant the lines, doubling and quadrupling the tempo.

The Vyas (Director), in white turban, tunic, and dhoti,
stands near the characters and openly prompts them. Every

character speaks in monosyllabic or split monosyllabic speech, drawling the words so that they are stretched and made clear. The speeches take three times as long as it would take to say them normally. Even when a character is in a rage, or in a hurry, he speaks in monosyllables. For example, Sita says: "Kindly proceed quickly to the forest to gather fruits." Her delivery would be: "Kind-ly-ey pro-o-ce-eed qui-ick-le-ey to-oo the-ee fo-res-t to-oo gaa-ther frui-ts."

If an important dialogue or a message or a decisive sentence is spoken by a principal character, it is preceded by a loud ejaculation by the Vyas: "*Bol sia pati rama chandra ki jai!*" ("Shout Raja Rama Chandra's victory!"), or "*Bol janaka-*

dulari ki jai!" ("Shout victory to Sita, daughter of King Janaka!")—and the audience roars in a chorus the last word of the Vyas. Sometimes an enthusiastic spectator shouts a slogan in praise of Rama, and the rest of the crowd joins in. This breaks the monotony and enlivens the spectators, uniting the audience and making them concentrate on a single point. It acts as a full stop to the speech dialogue and is a signal for a new turn in the plot development. Or it may be only to hush the babble of the crowd.

On the tenth day of the moon (preceded by Navratri, nine nights of celebrations) the Dashahara festival concludes. Bright-painted cardboard effigies of the ten-headed Ravana, his younger brother Kumbhakarna (who slept for six months and woke up for one day only), his son Meghanada, and the demoness Taraka stand in the arena. Rama and Lakshmana move about with rhythmic steps shooting arrows at the effigies as the public shouts slogans of their victory. At sunset Rama's fiery arrows hit the effigies, which explode in fireworks. The people return home with a feeling of moral victory.

MAKE-UP AND COSTUME

All the parts are acted by men. Rama, Lakshmana, Bharata, Shatrughna, and Sita are played by boys under fourteen. Although they were of the Sun dynasty of the Kshatriyas, the boys playing the roles are from Brahmin families. The actor playing Rama must be pure, innocent, and have no knowledge of sex. His hands and legs are striped with sandalwood paste, so that from a distance he looks as if he is wearing stockings and gloves up to the elbow. His forehead, smeared with holy powder, has yellow lines drawn vertically and a U-shaped white insignia with a flamelike mark in the center. His eyelids are mascaraed and his eyelashes silvered. A jeweled drop dangles from his nose. On both cheeks flowerlike round patterns made of aluminum stars give luster to his face. His

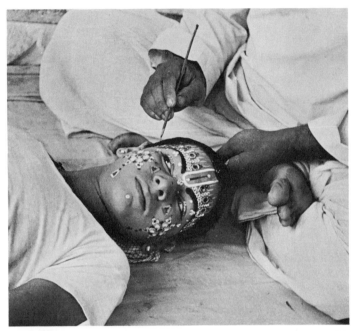

Rama lying flat on the ground while being made up for the Ramlila in Ramnagar

costume is completed with necklaces of many sizes, a silver-laced jacket, and a saffron silk dhoti. When the young boy puts on the gilded crown, the spirit of the god enters his body.

Different make-up men take care of different characters. Rama, Lakshmana, and Sita are attended by a group that helps them with make-up, costumes, and properties. For Rama's make-up, one man is in charge of his crown, and another of his bows and arrows; one paints him with sandalwood paste; one fixes shining aluminum specks on his cheeks; and one fans him with a bushy fly whisk. Some of these devotional attendants are hereditary and charge no money.

The other characters are played by adult males. A man playing Bali may act the role for ten years, Ravana for twenty years, Hanuman for thirty years. Their costumes, jewelry, and masks are fashioned by expert craftsmen for whom this is an opportunity to display their art. Ravana's ten-headed mask

Rama and Lakshmana sitting cross-legged as they check their make-up. Behind them is the gray-bearded Baba Ram Lakhan Das, who has been playing Hanuman for the last forty years

has a silver lining with a black woolen weave and is an awesomely heavy headgear. The actor sometimes takes it off during the performance. When his turn comes to perform, he adjusts the mask and again is the haughty demon who stamps and romps. The most venerable mask is that of Hanuman. The one used in the Ramnagar Ramlila is made of almost ten pounds of copper painted shining red with black curled mustaches. A fifty-eight-year-old gray-bearded man, Baba Ram Lakhan Das, has been playing the role for forty years. Now he is known by the name of Hanuman. Characters playing Dasaratha, Ravana, Janaka, and Jatayu shed their original names and become known by their Ramlila names.

All these people believe in their roles. The man playing the role must be a devotee of the god. During the performance the self-hypnotized actor feels superhuman power. Once in the mid-nineteenth century an English priest made fun of an actor playing Hanuman and remarked that, while Hanuman could jump over the sea with a single leap, the actor could not even jump over the Varana stream. The devotee actor was so incensed that he accepted the challenge. He stood on a mound by the bank of the Varana and jumped over the stream. The effort was too much for him, and he died on the spot. The mask of this actor has been preserved

Rama and Sita made up for the Ramlila in Ramnagar. Rama's crown has not yet been put on. He wears a jeweled drop in his nose, and Sita wears a large nose ring

Hanuman's mask being fixed by a holy man during the enactment of Ramlila in Ramnagar

and is still worn by whoever plays the role of Hanuman at the Nati Imli Ramlila celebration.

The expenses of the Ramlila in different areas range from twelve hundred to three thousand rupees because most labor is free. Generally a Vyas with his team of Rama, Lakshmana, Sita, Hanuman, and one or two demon characters approaches a Ramlila committee which offers him dresses, crowns, masks, lighting facilities, arena stage, and platforms, plus a lump sum of five hundred to eight hundred rupees.

Amateur players join in as monkeys, soldiers, demons, courtiers, and people attending Sita's marriage and Rama's coronation. The Ramayanis (Chorus) are generally nonprofessionals. (Even off-season they sing the verses for their own enjoyment.) The people who carry Rama's throne on their shoulders are not paid. They do it out of devotion, like the thousands at Jagannath Puri who draw the holy chariot inspired by religious zeal.

Rama's fee could be 100 rupees for the entire Ramlila. Sita charges much less. Ravana's fee is equal to Rama's, sometimes more. Hanuman accepts a token fee because he is a devotee of Rama. A Brahmin actor is paid his regular fee plus the *dakshina*.*

Generally an actor starts his career by playing the youngest brother, Shatrughna. Then he is promoted to play Sita, and then Rama. When he has been groomed in the tradition and has become an adult, he plays Hanuman or a demon. Every night when Rama has completed his make-up and put on his crown in the dressing room, he is fed along with Sita and Lakshmana (also the other two brothers if they are playing that night) and worshiped ceremoniously by the *arati* lamps. After the performance the Swaroops (the Incarnations of the godly spirit: the four brothers and Sita) are conducted to the dressing room where they are again fed with milk and *pera* sweets. Rich families in the area consider it a great honor to feed the Swaroops. On the day of Rama's coronation the devotees offer gifts of shawls, saris, sweets, fruits, flowers, money, and ornaments, which are distributed among the Vyas, the Swaroops, and the other important players.

The celebrations of processions, street pageants, and the burning of effigies involve separate expenses. Effigies of Ravana and Kumbhakarna are fashioned by the traditional Muslim craftsmen. A good Ravana, which nods its head, parts its lips, and rolls its eyes, and is loaded with fireworks and firecrackers, costs about five hundred rupees.

---

* When a Brahmin is invited to dinner or to conduct a religious ceremony, he expects to be paid the *dakshina*—a fee. It has the sanction of a religious convention of centuries. Even the gods are bound by it.

Different localities specialize in different scenes.

The Chitrakut Ramlila at Chauka Ghat starts with the banishment of Rama and continues for fifteen nights. It is an enactment without speech. The action is focused on one climactic moment. It is a kind of tableau with limited action accompanied by music. The story is divided into different scenes, each lasting about an hour. For example, the scene is Sita's abduction: Sita is alone in the hut after she has sent Lakshmana away in search of Rama. Ravana enters in disguise and asks for alms but refuses to cross the "forbidding line" which Lakshmana had drawn for Sita around the hut. She comes out to give him alms. The moment she crosses the line, Ravana throws off his mask, appears in his own terrifying form, and carries her away. The *lila* is finished. In another scene Rama is resting at Sumeru Mountain. Nala and Nila, two blue-faced monkey engineers, fan him. Sugriva, the Monkey King, sits with Rama's head in his lap. Bibishana, who has walked over from Ravana's camp, is bending over the resting Rama, whispering something in his ear. Angada and Hanuman are massaging his feet. Jambavan, the wise King of the Bears, sits quietly. Lakshmana is alert with his bow and arrow guarding the camp. The scene is a silent picture which the spectators watch for about an hour. At the end Rama gets up, and the performance is over.

Chauka Ghat's specialty is Rama's return journey to Ayodhya. Rama, Lakshmana, Sita, Hanuman, and others, seated on a thirty-foot-high *pushp-viman* (flower-decked throne), are carried on the shoulders of an army of devotees. Two fireworks men walk ahead holding red and white flaming torches fixed on long poles. Occasionally firecrackers erupt, scattering red and green lights in the dark. Magnesium wires burn brightly, dazzling the eyes of Rama, Lakshmana, and Sita. The milling crowd surges. The *pushp-viman* moves forward, backward, dashes forward, and the crowd shouts slogans of Rama's victory. After five hours, at two in the morning, the procession reaches its destination, hardly a mile from its starting point. This is the most sought-after float in Varanasi.

Nati Imli is famous for Bharata Milap (the meeting of the four brothers after Rama returns home victorious). Three hundred thousand people attend this glorious pageant. Roads, roofs, balconies, and distant buildings are packed with people. In the square of Nati Imli, the ceremony takes place at exactly 4:45 in the afternoon. On a platform covered by a red cloth, marigolds and roses lie scattered. Bharata and Shatrughna, the two brothers, stand waiting for the arrival of Rama and Lakshmana.

The maharaja of Banaras enters the arena on his royal elephant followed by seven elephants covered with heavy brocade shawls. The people joyously shout for the maharaja, who on this occasion is considered the special representative of the god Shiva. His elephant raises its vermilion-painted trunk and salutes the people, then ambles to the other end of the square, where the maharaja receives the ovation with folded hands. The elephant returns to his place.

A few minutes later the *pushp-viman* arrives carried by Ahirs (members of the milkman community), wearing red turbans, white dhotis, and white shoulder-scarves. On the throne are seated Rama, Lakshmana, Sita, Hanuman, and others. Rama and Lakshmana climb down. Bharata and Shatrughna rush toward them as the crowd cheers for joy. It is a touching sight. The four brothers come together on the decorated platform and embrace each other. Four Vyases, masters of ceremony, dressed in white dhotis and gold-edged turbans, fan them with silken scarves. They face all four directions in turn. Finally the brothers stand in the center tightly clasping each other, their heads together. This ceremony lasts about fifteen minutes. Tears come to the eyes of the overjoyed people. A collective prayer of three hundred thousand people arises from the square. The pageant is a glorious spiritual experience. It releases the unconscious yearning connected with meetings and partings, in which life itself

*The maharaja of Banaras on his elephant as he greets the people
with folded hands during a Ramlila procession*

is a short meeting in the immense space of parting.

PAGEANT PROCESSION

The cycle plays are marked by three processions which
involve lavish display: Rama's marriage, Nak-kattaiya, and
Rama's return.

Rama's marriage and his return to Ayodhya start at nine
in the evening and finish at two in the morning. The two
processions are attended by gods, kings, monkeys, and generals seated on silver stools or in *tam-jhams* (ornate reclining
chairs in which one sits with the legs spread out). The characters wear brocade tunics, gold-laced slippers, pearl earrings,
necklaces, and masks. The Banka (a young boy wearing a
Rajput court dress) in a *tam-jham* is a glittering decoration.
He wears white *chooridars* (tight-fitted jodhpurs loosely

gathered below the knees), a brocade tunic, a plumed turban, and many jewels. He is a mannequin for the display of orna- ments. Rich landlords and wealthy houses find this an oc- casion to show their inherited jewels. Family bodyguards with swords walk by the side of the dressed-up Banka, who is car- ried by attendants. If diamond-studded jewelry is on display, he wears cream-colored dress; if it is a sapphire set, he is dressed in blue; if emeralds, he is in sparkling green.

Rama's marriage and return are celebrated with grandeur. Singers, dancers, and acrobats entertain the royal couple. Every form of entertainment is permissible on these occasions.

The most colorful procession is Nak-kattaiya (nak means nose, kattaiya means cutting off). Khara and Dushana, the demon brothers of Surpanakha, are marching with their army against Rama to avenge their disfigured sister.

The Chet Ganj area is famous for this procession, which lasts from eleven o'clock at night until six in the morning. One hundred thousand people participate. It is a procession of masked demons, gods, devils, acrobats, tumblers, accom- panied by the music of big drums and horns.

Surpanakha, Ravana's sister whose nose has been chopped off by Lakshmana, leads the procession. She wears a blue-black mask with a bloody hollow, carries a massive wooden flail in her hand, and walks defiantly. Demons in gruesome make-up follow her on horses, camels, and elephants.

A baffling item is the lag, which means a support. A man stands on a decorated wooden plank balancing another man on his outstretched hand. The second man balances a third man on the palm of his hand, an acrobatic feat that seems to defy the laws of gravity. But the secret is a steel rod hidden under the garments of the performing men which supports the entire weight. Credulous women and farmers believe that the man at the bottom has godly power. Floats of demons drinking blood, ogres wearing necklaces of skulls, and eunuchs singing and dancing with lewd gestures follow. The procession is an orgy of perversions. In the puritanical religious drama of Rama's life, it is a release for the common man's desire for vulgarity.

The goddess Kali appears in her two incarnations, the De- structive Kali and the Benevolent Durga. Kali has a huge, circular six-foot mask with a jet black face and a red tongue hanging out, and she holds a curved sword. Durga wears a triangular mask with a lemon-white face and carries a straight sword. Both express two facets of the same power: the terrible and the kind; the destructive and the boon giver; the killer and the reviver. A half dozen Durgas have sword fights with a half dozen Kalis. These duels are enacted in the narrow

Banaras lanes by men trained in swordsmanship. The long
winding procession crawls through many crossings which are
turned into arenas by the acrobats, tumblers, dancers, and
jousting demons. Kali and Durga, the Good and the Evil, are
two wills at war with each other. The two attack each other.
The fight always ends in a draw. The two forces are balanced.
Neither the Good nor the Evil triumphs. The crowd shouts:
"*Sanche darbar ki jai!*" (Victory to the court of truth!)

At the end of the procession is Khara-Dushana, two demon
brothers in one man. He wears a brass mask of an ass.

THE RAMNAGAR PAGEANT

The annual Ramlila at Ramnagar, twelve miles from Banaras across the Ganges, is a spectacular production. Before
Independence, Ramnagar State had a Ramlila Department
with a secretary-general and undersecretaries. One of the
clauses at the time of the merger provided that every year the
Uttar Pradesh government would set aside the sum of one
hundred thousand rupees for the Ramlila. Apart from this
subsidy, the maharaja spends large sums from his private purse
to celebrate this pageant. The royal armory, elephants, and
courtiers are at the service of the Ramlila.

The acting sites cover an area of a triangle of about three
square miles. The holy shrines, gardens, and temples in Ramnagar are named for places in the *Ramayana:* Ayodhya, Janakapuri, Chitrakut, Pampasar, Kishkindha, Panchavati, and
Lanka. They are reserved solely for the enactment of Ramlila
and are guarded all year.

The Ramlila opens with the birth of Rama and lasts thirty
days, ending approximately on the Ashwin Poornima with
Rama's coronation. On the last day, Rama, Lakshmana, and
Sita enter the courtyard of the maharaja's palace amidst cheer-
ing people, all seated according to class and status. The maharaja, dressed in a white dhoti tucked up at the knees in the
style of a common farmer, receives the trio and leads them to
the decorated throne where they sit accompanied by Bharata,
Shatrughna, and others. The maharaja squats on the floor and
offers worship to the Swaroops with the assistance of a Brahmin priest who pours holy water of the Ganges from a jar
while ringing a tiny bell. During this ceremony the Swaroops
are fed on palm leaves from silver bowls. After this, the maharaja gives *dakshina* to the participants and offers homage to
the gods.

The *lila* starts at five every evening and lasts until nine,
with a half-hour interval at sunset. The maharaja retires for
evening prayers, and Rama and Lakshamana are carried away
on Hanuman's shoulders to the retiring *ashram*, a temple or-

chard on one side. The congregation relaxes, buying sweetmeats, souvenirs, and masks from the lamplit stalls. Each day's
performance concludes with the thrilling *arati*. Burning magnesium wires light up the faces of Rama and Lakshmana.
The spluttering blazes heighten the tension of the scene.
Some spectators come for the *arati* alone.

No microphone is used even when five thousand spectators
attend. The semicircle of the squatting people is hemmed in
by a troupe of seven elephants who carry the maharaja's guests
and other important spectators. The royal elephant stands a
few steps ahead of the others and is distinguished by a canopied howdah on which the maharaja sits. The singing chorus
sits near the elephants. Everyone knows the words of the
song. The gold-dusted sky, the serene forest, and the pure
air create an atmosphere. Even when the spectators cannot
hear the lines or make out the actors clearly, they see the play
because it is being enacted in their minds.

Wrestling bouts, swordfights, acrobatics, and tumbling add
excitement to the pageant. During the final combat, Rama
and Ravana stand on two sides of the rectangular arena. Ravana's chariot is drawn by blue cardboard horses and Rama's
by milk-white ones. The chief director (Vyas) and his two
assistants in white dhotis run about the stage prompting and
helping the combatants.

Raghunath Datt Sharma has acted as the chief Vyas for the
last ten years: He said: "Rama, Lakshmana, and Sita do not
know when and where to speak. I am here at their service,
like the charioteer who guided the valiant Arjuna, telling him
when to shoot the arrow and in which direction."

When Rama was asked to take off his crown for a photograph, the head priest thundered a rebuke: "It is not a drama,
but an act of faith! Once Rama puts on the crown, nobody
can take it off. He is the god. Who are you to ask the god to
remove his headgear?"

While Hanuman, Ravana, and Jatayu play their roles for
years, Rama, Sita, and the three brothers are changed every
third year. They are rehearsed for about two months by the
Vyas, but young players cannot memorize a drama lasting for
thirty days. The Vyas prompts them constantly in full public
view. If Rama forgets his lines, the Vyas speaks them loudly
and Rama takes them up. While speaking his lines Rama does
not show any expression. He does not move. He is detached.
He does not act. He is unconcerned, lost in the ceremony. He
looks like a young prince being crowned. There is so much awe
of Rama's godhood that in spite of the noise the boy actor's
piping voice is heard by thousands. The spectators have heard
these words many times. They have grown up listening to them

in the street plays, in narrative poems, in chanting on the ghats. The Ramlila only confirms what is already familiar. Some devoted spectators sit with eyes shut, "watching" the performance.

This ritualistic presentation, almost dehumanized and devoid of theatrical realism, has glorious spurts of realistic effects. While the scenes of Dasaratha's pangs and the long discourses on religious philosophy are at times dull to watch, the scenes of crossing the river, Sita's marriage, setting the Golden Lanka on fire, and Rama's coronation are pageants of splendor.

Sita's marriage is celebrated in Janakapuri in the Vedic tradition. About ten thousand people attend. At the sacrificial fire sandalwood is burned and clarified butter is poured as the Vedic hymns are chanted. The maharaja's courtiers attend, dressed in gold-laced turbans and stiff brocade tunics. When Rama lifts Shiva's bow, plucks the cord, and breaks the bow, it is timed with the firing of a cannon, and the thunder is heard for ten miles around. Tulsidas, while describing the breaking of Shiva's bow, says that the sound was so terrifying that the frightened elephants trumpeted and the horses of the Sun God fled in all directions. The realistic enactment is born out of the belief that everything present is the incarnation of a spiritual reality which must manifest itself in the physical.

Similarly, when Rama, Lakshmana, and Sita are rowed across the river by Guha, the king of ferrymen, the scene is enacted by the side of a little stream, just as a film is shot "on location." The Ksheera Sagar (Ocean of Milk) takes place in a huge water tank where Vishnu lies in repose on the coils of Sheshanag (the mythical Cobra), shaded by his hood. Setting the Golden Lanka on fire draws more than twenty thousand people. The spectators are devout believers in the celebration.

This form of Ramlila was started by Maharaja Udita Narayan Singh about 125 years ago. The devout maharaja used to attend the Ramlila celebration at Banaras every year. Once the Crown Prince Ishwari Narayan Singh fell so ill that there was no hope for his recovery. The maharaja was greatly perturbed. That evening, when he went to attend the Ramlila, the spiritual head of the celebrations offered him a garland worn by Rama and asked him to put it on the ailing prince. The prince recovered. From then on the maharaja became a devotee of Ramlila and Tulsidas. He decided to propagate the *Ramayana* in two ways: by making available the meaning of the *Ramayana* to the common man through its enactment in the form of a spectacular Ramlila, and by having Tulsidas' *Ramacharitmanas* compiled in a massive illustrated book of five volumes 18½ by 14 inches. Famous artists of Rajasthan were invited to do the illustrations. They were done in Rajput style, showing many

locales and different actions in a single painting. Real sap-
phires, topazes, emeralds, rubies, and diamonds were powdered
and used to color the paintings, which are still amazingly fresh.
The volumes lie in the royal archives.

The maharaja's son, Ishwari Narayan Singh, perfected the
staging of Ramlila. He had scholars write a commentary on
Ramacharitmanas. A patron of art and culture, Maharaja Ishwari Narayan Singh trained students and established the tradition of chanting and enacting. He was the first Vyas. Some
of his famous pupils were Ram Ghulamji, Bandhan Pathak,
and Chhakan Lal. They in turn taught the art to their pupils
and carried the tradition further.

The present maharaja, Vibhuti Narayan Singh, a young
man of pure habits, maintains the tradition. He talks warmly
about this religious pageant. He believes that the festival has
bound the people of all castes and creeds into one single body,
experiencing the same spiritual joy. When he was asked, "Why
does a young boy always play Rama?" he replied: "Ramlila is
not a play, it is a *yagna*. A *yagna* has a different purpose. It is to
propitiate the gods so that the people in Ramnagar shall live
in peace and prosperity. A twelve-year-old boy is pure. The god
can enter only a pure body. A young boy is detached; so is
Rama. Therefore only an innocent boy can play Rama in this
yagna."

Ramlila in Varanasi is not a dramatic spectacle, it is a ritual.
It is an expression of the whole life of the people: their cus-

toms, beliefs, crafts, arts, philosophy, poetry, music, even their wealth and valor.

Earlier *lila* plays were of many types: Harishchandralila was about the truthful ancient Hindu king Harishchandra, who in order to keep his word of honor had to sell his wife and act as a slave in a cremation ground; Dhruvlila dealt with the life of the boy-saint Dhruv; Prahladlila narrated the incidents in the life of the boy-prince Prahlad, who refused to accept his father as the god and became a boy-saint. Of the many traditional *lilas* only Krishnalila and Narasimhalila have survived. These are one-day pageants enacted every year, not regular cycle plays.

With its rich tradition of pageant and color, Varanasi gave many playwrights to Hindi. Famous ones are Bharatendu Harishchandra, father of Hindi drama, whose verse plays and pungent farces portray the seamy side of Kashi with its glorious spiritualism; Agha Hashar Kashmiri, Raunaq Banarsi, Vinayak Prasad Talib, and Mian Zarif, darlings of the Parsi theatrical companies; Jaishankar Prasad, the towering literary figure of the twenties; and Munshi Premchand, the greatest Hindi nov-

The furious Parasurama, a famous Ramlila character, played by the seventy-year-old Baba Santa in a Punjab town

elist. Today half a dozen amateur groups are struggling. Their acting is crude and their stage presentation poor. It is the Ramlila that represents Varanasi's passion for pageant, music, acting, poetry, philosophy, display, and showmanship.

Tulsidas' *Ramacharitmanas* can be understood by a common man in the Varanasi area even today, but in other parts of North India it has an archaic flavor. In different periods local playwrights have written the *Ramayana* in simple Hindi, Urdu, and regional dialects and have popularized the Ramlila tradition. In Delhi, Punjab, and Rajasthan, it is staged either on platforms in the open in folk style or on a proscenium stage.

The presentation of Ramlila on a proscenium stage in the towns is a mixture of the folk theater with some elements of the classical and a dash of the Western. The crudely painted drop curtain generally shows King Dasaratha's court or Rama and Sita sitting on a canopied throne. The orchestra, made up of a harmonium master, a violinist, a flutist, and a drummer, is seated in the pit. The play opens with the explosion of a firecracker. The curtain rises, revealing the entire cast (all males) in complete make-up, standing with hands folded and eyes shut, singing the *mangalacharana* (prayer song) in a classical *raga*. The play rambles on from nine at night to two in the morning, telling a portion of the story with a great deal of singing, dancing, and bombastic dialogue, and many sword-fights, comic interludes, and tableaux.

In some productions a man sits on the stage chanting snatches from *Ramacharitmanas*, which lies open before him on a low sandalwood stool. When he sings, the action on the stage stops. The singing comments on, illustrates, and externalizes the feeling of the characters, who act out silently or in simple prose what the singer recites. When Sita looks at Rama for the first time in her palace garden she does not utter a word. Her thoughts are expressed by the singer. Or when Rama, Lakshmana, and Sita are leaving Ayodhya for the jungles, beginning their fourteen-year banishment, and bidding farewell to their family, the action on the stage is silently carried out while the singer chants the feelings of the characters. This adds a dimension to the performance.

In North India there is no professional theatrical company. The religious festival of Ramlila is the biggest factor in continuing the dramatic tradition and is more powerful in its sweep than any other folk theater. It reaches the farthest village, touches every home, and is the most electrifying influence on the cultural life of the people.

Chapter Seven

RASLILA

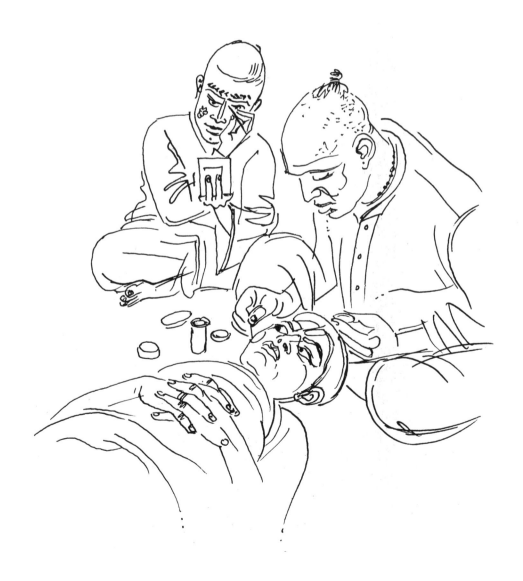

THE POPULAR love story of Krishna and Radha finds expression throughout India. The devotees of Krishna include the Ras dancers of Gujarat and Saurashtra, the Krishnattam actors of Kerala, the graceful *nayikas* (heroines) of the Manipuri dance in the Assam Hills, the Pala singer-actors of Bengal and Orissa, and the Krishnalila and Raslila performers of the Ganges Valley.

The Kathak dancers of North India specialize in the Radha-Krishna love legend in their highly sensuous dance. The courtesans of Banaras and Lucknow have entertained audiences with the love pangs of Krishna and Radha for centuries. The Kangra school of painting is filled with Krishna-Radha lore. Sculptors, potters, embroiderers, and weavers have celebrated Krishna. Krishna and Radha are important factors in the spiritual unity of India.

Krishna is the most human of Hindu gods. He is a lover, a mischief-maker, a statesman, a yogi. While Rama is a preserver of tradition, Krishna is a breaker of it. He steals butter, teases milkmaids, lies to his mother, fights against demons, and kills his power-drunk uncle, King Kamsa. He is the pivotal character in the *Mahabharata* battle. He sides with the Pandavas and inspires Arjuna to fight while he himself remains detached. His philosophical discourse on the battlefield, in which he preached action without involvement, resulted in the *Bhagavad Gita*, the holy book of Hindus.

In the *Mahabharata* Krishna's image emerges as that of a warrior, philosopher, and statesman. By the sixth century the myth of Radha, as an object of spiritual love, was added to the Krishna lore. The Sanskrit poet Jayadeva of Bengal in his *Geetagovinda* (twelfth century) wrote erotic songs about Radha and Krishna. In the fifteenth and sixteenth centuries the Vaishnava movement, a reaction against hardened ritualistic Hinduism, swept the country, expressing itself in devotional singing and dancing. Saints, poets, and singers added physical glamour to the spiritual love of Radha and Krishna.

Raslila, an operatic play, deals with Krishna's life. Its homeland is Braj Bhoomi, an eighty-four-square-mile area eighty miles southeast of New Delhi which has continued the tradition for over three hundred years. Braj Bhoomi includes Mathura, Vrindaban, Gokul, Nandgaon, Govardhan, and Barsana, all places connected with Krishna's childhood. Krishna was born in Mathura behind the doors of the jail where his parents were imprisoned by his uncle, King Kamsa; he was raised in Gokul across the river Jamuna by his foster parents, father Nanda and mother Yashoda; he tended cattle in Vrindaban; he waited for Radha who came to see him from Barsana; he protected the cattle and the people of the area from a torrential downpour by lifting Mount Govardhan on his little finger.

The area has more than eight hundred public temples devoted to Krishna. Among the famous ones are the Dwarkadhish temple, Shahaji's marble temple, and Ranganath temple (built in the last century by merchants and princes in commemoration of their religious guru Swami Rangacharya). This last has seven concentric courtyards, and in the innermost shrine a sandalwood pillar covered with 12½ maund (1,025 pounds) of gold plate. An estate of 360 villages was dedicated to the temple. Today the expenses of maintaining a huge staff and daily meals for hundreds of Brahmins and sadhus are met by this estate.

Every street in Vrindaban has a temple; every home has a niche for Krishna's image. His life, every trait of his character, every achievement, every place associated with him has been described. Of all the gods, Krishna has the largest number of names: Devaki Nandan (son of Devaki), Ghanashyam (dark cloud), Nanda Nandan (Nanda's son), Radha Vallabh (Radha's lord), Yashoda Nandan (Yashoda's son), Shyam (the dark-bodied), Yogi Raj (the king yogi), Gopal (tender of cows), Shyam Sundar (the beautiful dark), Bansi Dhar (holder of the flute), Manamohan (winner of the mind), Giridhari (lifter of a mountain), and so on. The names could easily fill a small-town telephone directory.

Braj Bhoomi is a totally agricultural area. Not only is it strictly vegetarian, but even onions and garlic are banned in the houses of good Hindus there. It follows the Krishna cult; and it speaks the mellifluous Braj language which became the pan-Indian language of devotional songs, philosophical discussions, and spiritual seminars between the twelfth and eighteenth centuries.

The Braj language has pathos and sweetness. Saint-poets described their spiritual quests in this language. Namadeva of Maharashtra (fourteenth century) and Guru Nanak, founder of the Sikh faith (fifteenth century), wrote superb religious poetry in it. Rahim Khan, courtier to Akbar the Great; Surdas, the Hindi bard; and Bihari, the singer of sensuous beauty, composed immortal verses in Braj.

In the sixteenth century, gurus from Bengal, Rajasthan, South India, and Maharashtra came to this land and made it a center of religious philosophy. Vallabhacharya, the Telugu saint from South India, settled there and preached the Pushti cult, one form of attaining god in Vaishnavism. His pupil Surdas (1479–1584), along with seven contemporary saint-poets called "Ashta Chhap" (the club of eight devotee poets, all disciples of Vallabhacharya), left behind unusually brilliant poetry. Surdas, who in his youth fell in love with a prostitute and became disillusioned about worldly desires, turned to spiritual bliss. Tortured by guilt, he plucked out his eyes and roamed as a blind bard singing of Krishna's childhood. In pathos and in the vivid details of a child's life, his devotional poetry is unsurpassed in the whole of Indian literature.

Vallabhacharya was the father of Pushti Marg, a spiritual path of life, in which the devotee worships Krishna as a wife loves her husband; this is possible only through the *pushti* (grace) of the god. Devotional worship flourished throughout Bengal, South India, and in the Ganges Valley in the sixteenth and seventeenth centuries. It found expression in Keertans (community singing), *lilas* (plays), and Raslilas (operatic plays) in which Krishna becomes the husband and all the devotees become Gopis (female companions) searching for him. In the Seva Padhati cult, prevalent in Gujarat and Saurashtra, followers dress the image of the god in clothes, adorn it with ornaments, rock it on a decorated swing, and offer it food. After this the devotee eats. The Sakhi Bhava is practiced in Orissa by men. The devotee becomes a female friend of the god, his beloved wife. To mark his devotion, he even wears a sari and a blouse and adopts feminine mannerisms. For four days a month he remains secluded in a corner of the house, as a woman in a Brahmin household does during her menstrual period.

The Bhakti cult made music and dance an essential part of its offering. Shankaradeva of Assam (a saint-poet of the six-

Krishna and Radha on their throne attended by the Gopis

teenth century) carried this to the extreme by making dance-music-drama the sole medium of spiritual offering. His Ankia Nats (one-act plays), theatrically exciting, have been played for four centuries in monasteries and temples. Shankaradeva's books are worshiped in the monasteries where monks chant and sing and dance the master's devotional works.

The Vaishnava movement was responsible for the introduction of the ras by Maharaja Bhagyachandra (eighteenth century), a devotee of Krishna, into Manipur State where it has been a living tradition of the people's worship ritual ever since. It is performed on six occasions a year, of which the most colorful is Vasanta Ras at Holi, the festival of colors in spring. Krishna dances with Chandrabali, making Radha extremely jealous. Casting off her veil, symbol of her love, Radha goes away. Krishna is disturbed. He goes in search of her and finds her. She spurns him. He seeks her forgiveness. Ultimately the two join. The finale is a circular dance in which Radha and Krishna are the central figures.

The dancer wears a stiff, bulging skirt adorned with pieces of mirror and with a velvet hem. Her hair is rolled up in a bun adorned with flower wreaths. Her face, dotted with sandalwood paste and sprayed with mica, is covered by a maikhum, a gauze veil tucked up into her conical bun. The face is expressionless, like glazed porcelain. She dances with her head tilted, gliding in a dream.

The dance is accompanied by drums, flutes, cymbals, conch-shells, and pena (a string instrument made of horse-tail hairs strung on a bamboo stick).

In the Braj area Raslila is a highly developed form of dance-drama, different in treatment, style, and dress from that of Manipur. Mahatma Dhruvadas Ji Maharaj (sixteenth century), a Braj Bhoomi poet, wrote forty-two lilas on Krishna's life. Some of these contain erotic symbolism. One of the couplets says: "These friends have decorated the room with flowers and scents. Radha and Krishna both are young and expert in sexual play." Vishwanath Chakravarti, the noted Sanskrit commentator on Shrimad Bhagavata Purana (an eighth-century book of tales of Vishnu and Krishna in particular), says: "Ras is a combination of dance, lyrics, kisses, embraces, etc." Parmanand Das, the saint-poet of the Ashta Chhap group, remarks: "Ras consists of embraces, kisses, physical intimacy."

The word ras is traced to many sources. The Sanskrit word rasa means "flavor, enjoyment, blissful state." Ras transports the spectator-listeners to a blissful state. In Rajasthan the rasak was a one-act play with five characters. Jain literature is full of religious rasaks. The word has also been associated with raso,

meaning the biography of a king in verse describing his valor and exploits in war. A famous one is *Prithiraj* Raso* by Chand Bardai. In the Braj language *raso* means "quarrel." The quarrel of the spiritual and the physical, Krishna and the Gopis, has a shade of meaning in this local word. Some connect it with the Sanskrit word *rahas*, which means "secret communion"; the union of Radha and Krishna is a secret experience, a rare spiritual revelation that only a few people can share. With use *ras* has come to mean the love dance of Krishna with the Gopis and Radha, symbolizing the god and the devotees.

The legend of Krishna's dance and sport with the Gopis by the river Jamuna was an accepted concept. The tenth book of *Shrimad Bhagavata Purana* describes Maha Ras (the great *ras*) in which Krishna multiplies himself into as many Krishnas as there are Gopis seeking him and dances with them.

Raslila has devotional color. Three inspired saints—Narayan Bhatt, Ghumand Dev, and Hitharivansh—are said to have originated it. They took the neglected folk form and polished its music; devised its costumes, dance sequences, and ritualistic preliminaries; and established it as a dance opera.

* The Hindu king Prithviraj Chauhan, who was betrayed by his younger brother Jai Chand and thus defeated by the Muslim conqueror Shihab-ud-din (known as Muhammad of Ghor) in 1192.

A permanent stage built for Raslila on the bank of the holy river Jamuna. The flag shows the ancient Hindu swastika symbol

As it is performed today, Raslila has two parts: ras, the dance, and lila, the play. The program lasts three hours. One third is devoted to the ras, the preliminaries danced and sung by Krishna, Radha, and the Gopis. This is followed by the lila, a flowing story sung out by the Swami (the leader of the chorus) with other characters who improvise in prose.

One of the three most famous Raslilas is *Daan Lila*, in which Krishna teases the Gopis and insists that they pay a toll of milk and butter before he lets them go.

In *Nauka Lila* the Gopis want to cross the river Jamuna. It is late evening. They look for a boatman. No one is available. At last they see a boatman and shout for him, but he refuses to carry them. They beg. He agrees, but wants to be sure that the weight of the passengers will not overturn the boat. As he takes hold of each Gopi and lifts her to judge her weight, the Gopis recognize him as Krishna.

In *Uddhava Lila*, Krishna's minister-friend Uddhava believes in the abstract reality of the god, whereas Krishna's devotees believe in his physical incarnation. Uddhava always taunts Krishna about the Gopis who wait for his return to Gokul. Krishna sends Uddhava to Gokul to explain the futility of physical love. Uddhava is deeply moved by the love of Radha, Yashoda, and the Gopis and realizes the supremacy of their devotion.

THE STAGE

Raslila is enacted in the temple courtyard. It is intimate and demands reverence of the audience. Tamasha, Bhavai, and Nautanki cater to much larger audiences. They are secular and full of fun and noise. Staged in the village square, they are frequently interrupted by whistles and catcalls from the spectators. In contrast the puritanical Raslila *mandalis* (troupes) in Vrindaban consider it sacrilegious to perform in the street.

The audience, the musicians, and the characters cannot sit with their backs toward Krishna and Radha. The Gopis, after they whirl around in a dance sequence, always face Krishna and Radha.

The stage is divided into two parts: *singhasan*, the throne on which Krishna and Radha sit; and *ras asthan*, the acting area, which is one foot lower. The *pichhvai*, the backdrop, is a crudely painted curtain usually showing lotus flowers and swans in a pond. The musicians sit in a semicircle between the audience and the acting area. The squatting audience must leave their shoes outside in the care of a watchman. No one can smoke or even drink water during a Raslila. Their mouths must be "pure."

The orchestra consists of four instruments: cymbals, hand drum, harmonium, and *sarangi*. The Swami (leader of the troupe) is the principal singer and may also play one of the instruments. Other members of the orchestra are called the Samajis. They join the refrain, take up the song to give the Swami some rest, and sometimes act in the *lila*.

The Swami, always a Brahmin priest, is well versed in Sanskrit, scriptures, classical and folk music, rituals, and literature on the love of Krishna and Radha. He does not have a promp-

ter's book. He weaves into the text snatches from ancient Sanskrit works, and references, quotations, and extracts from the entire Braj literature. If the audience is enthusiastic and gifts are offered to him at the climactic moments, he lengthens the *lila*. He has a fabulous memory. Without breaking form, structure, or theme, he can make the texture artistically rich.

THE PERFORMANCE

Two stagehands, sometimes the musicians, hold a bright silk embroidered curtain, then whisk it away revealing a tableau: Krishna and Radha seated on the throne, the Gopis standing three on each side. The Swami declaims, "Shout the Victory of Lord Krishna!" and the audience responds. He goes forward, touches the feet of Radha and Krishna, passes his hands over his eyes, incorporating their grace, and returns to his seat, walking backward.

He sings the *vandana* (prayer song) first in Sanskrit and then in Braj, in praise of his guru, then of Vrindaban land. He chants the glory of Krishna and sings a devotional hymn to Radha. Then he sings to both of them. Each Samaji sings a prayer song in praise of Krishna and Radha. During eight or ten such songs Krishna sits on the throne with his arm around Radha's neck.

This is followed by the *arati*. The Gopis hold a large, brass plate containing small lighted lamps made of flour paste and filled with ghee. As they sing they rotate this clockwise before the faces of Radha and Krishna. The *arati* plate is circulated among the audience, who pass their hands over the sacred flame, imbibe the light, and leave money offerings.

One of the Gopis folds her hands before Radha and Krishna and says: "Hay priya pritam ji! It is time for your daily *ras*. Kindly come to the sacred dance arena."

Krishna begs Radha to step down to the arena.

Radha grasps Krishna's hand, gets up, lets go of his hand, and recites a couplet: "I have great temptation for the *ras* and for the union. Let's go to some new bower along with the Gopis."

She puts her arm around Krishna's neck and steps down from the throne. Krishna stands in his characteristic pose playing the flute, his right foot crossed in front of his left at the ankle. Radha stands facing him with her back toward the audience. The six Gopis flank them. They dance slowly in a circle, singing a song. Then they leave the song and quicken the tempo. The Swami speaks out the drum syllables: *ta-dhin ta-dhin, tat-tat thai thai....* They whirl and jump forward into the ring and then jump backward and hop on the floor in a crouching posture, their saris spread out. Krishna and Radha

dance separately and then together. At climactic moments
Krishna performs acrobatic jumps. The people shower flowers
and rose petals and shout: "Radhaiaiai . . . Shyam!" The devotees believe that those who do not join in this holy slogan
will be born dumb in their next life, and that those who do not
clap in rhythm will be crippled.

The dance includes chakkars, torahs, and tihais—specialties
of the classical Kathak style. Chakkars are whirling movements.
Torah is a composition of rhythmic syllables. Tihai is the three-
line repetition of a phrase of rhythmic syllables used to adorn
the concluding part of a torah. The basic rhythmic pattern
in Kathak stemmed from the decorative dance interludes which
are so much a part of the ras performance; thus the rhythmic
sequences such as paran and paramulu used in Kathak are borrowed from ras. The basic stance of a Kathak dancer is with the
left arm up vertically and the right kept at shoulder level
bending forward at the elbow, the fingers of both hands deco-
ratively extended. In Raslila, Krishna often strikes this pose.

The *torah* has two types of rhythmic syllable-speech, one of the drum, the other of the feet, both synchronized. In one commonly performed *torah* the feet produce these rhythmic notes: tat/tat/tathai/thaitat/tathai/thaitat/tatra/amta/thai—/tatra/amta/thai/—/tatra/amta/thai. The drum speaks out the same *torah* in these syllables: dha/dha/dhadhin/dhindha/nadhin/dhindha/ tirkit/tirkit/thai/—/tirkit/tirkit/thai/—/tirkit/tirkit/thai.

At the end, the rhythmic syllables: tat/tat/thai/—/are repeated three times, synchronized with the foot beat in a triple flourish. The final *thai* is the conclusion of the rhythmic phrase and is a signal for the players to return to their respective positions. Radha and Krishna sit back on their throne. A curtain is drawn. This concludes the *ras*.

The Swami sings the devotional hymn: "Radhey-Radhey-Govind, Govind-Radhey." The Samajis and the audience join in. Some devotee, a bearded sadhu or a close-shaven priest, comes into the area zealously clanging large metal tongs studded with brass bells and chanting the words. The audience claps in time with his chant, losing itself in the *dhun* (the melody). As the tempo rises, he grows more and more vigorous. He is possessed and makes the audience possessed. At a peak of excitement all together stand up and rock and sway their arms overhead, clapping rhythmically and shouting the melody in quick gasps. This binds the devotee to the Lord Krishna.

Audience participation is a feature of Keertan singing. It was effectively used as a political weapon by the Rashtriya

Sewa Sangh (R.S.S.) during the Partition. The R.S.S. held chanting meetings at night. They sang and danced the "Rad-hey-Radhey-Govind" melody with such religious fervor that the people lost their identity to the leader-chanter, a political whip.

During the rhythmic chanting, a tableau is generally arranged behind the curtain.

At the climax of the chanting the curtain is removed and a tableau is revealed, a beautiful pictorial vision of Radha and Krishna. The leader shouts an elongated slogan, "*Radhaiaiai* . . . ," and the audience answers, ". . . *Shyam!*" This transforms the acting arena into a temple where Krishna and Radha, represented by two innocent boys, are the object of worship. Incense is burnt, and gifts and money are offered.

Two stagehands (sometimes taken from the devotee-audience) pick up the small silk curtain, which is always lying available on one side with the singing chorus, and draw it across the stage.

Krishna walks to the dressing room along with Radha and the Gopis. There he is offered fruit, milk, and sweets brought in by the devotees. He eats a bit. The leftover *pera* sweets are the blessed *prashad* which the devotees take and eat avidly. The Gopis eat after Krishna has been fed. The Swami bows, touching Krishna's feet, and receives the remaining food to be distributed among the singing chorus and other devotees.

After a brief interval the *lila* starts.

THE LILA

Almost every incident in Krishna's life has been turned into a *lila*. The most poignant is *Uddhava Lila*, which combines philosophy, love, pathos. The audience invariably weeps when the Gopis speak of their love pangs and Yashoda, Krishna's foster mother, describes how she fed Krishna, washed him, dressed him, rebuked him, and embraced him.

The Swami sings out the famous verses of the saint Kumbhandas (one of the eight saint-poets of Ashta Chhap in the fifteenth and sixteenth centuries), telling of how the Gopis are pining for Krishna. The Gopis and Radha are searching for Krishna. Radha asks the river Jamuna about his whereabouts. One of the Gopis replies that he has left Gokul and gone to Mathura. Both of them sing Surdas' lines, "Our eyes shed tears day and night." The evocative appeal of these verses is untranslatable.

The following scene shows Krishna's royal palace. In a series of stylized speeches he recalls Braj, his flute, Radha, the Gopis, the cows, Yashoda, and Nanda Baba. His minister-friend Uddhava is proud of his knowledge of the all-pervading Brahma and is a believer in the absolute concept of God. In order to cure him of his conceit, Krishna sends him to Gokul with his message.

Since there is a lot of singing in Uddhava's role, it is played by the Swami. During Krishna's soliloquy of song and speech, the Swami goes to the dressing room to make up and soon appears in the garb of Uddhava, wearing a bright yellow satin tunic, orange dhoti, and embroidered silk shawl. Krishna and Uddhava converse. Krishna describes his painful separation from his beloved people in Gokul and how he is tortured by his memories of them.

Prose dialogue is spoken in a stylized way, with every word broken into monosyllables or half-syllables. The dialogue between Krishna and Uddhava is about the supreme Knowledge of Life. Which is greater, attachment or detachment? Which is higher, the abstract image of God or the concrete?

Krishna sings out his message to Yashoda—a heart-rending poetical piece. The boy playing Krishna suddenly abandons his unrealistic acting and stylized speech and gives a highly realistic performance. After singing every two lines, he repeats them in prose. His eyes are full of tears, his throat is choked, his face is twisted with pain. The song concludes with two very touching lines for Radha: "You have turned me out of Braj. But, Radha, do not turn me out of your heart!"

Uddhava takes the message and goes to Braj. In actual presentation Krishna leaves the stage, and Uddhava remains. He cuts a circle on the stage, and this signifies that he has reached Gokul. There he meets Yashoda, who is waiting for Krishna,

A nineteenth-century temple wall hanging (kalamkari) showing Krishna, his foster mother Yashoda, and neighbors. Photograph courtesy of the National Museum, New Delhi

believing that he has only gone to play by the bank of the
Jamuna and will return any minute. Uddhava gives her his
greetings and wonders why she is pining for Krishna—the detached god, the Abstract. He talks of the philosophy of Brahma,
which preaches that the god pulsates in every leaf, in every
blade of grass, in every grain of sand. Yashoda replies by talking
about the physical image of the child Krishna.

Uddhava goes to the Gopis and chides them for falling in
love with the physical image of Krishna. He advises them to
meditate on the Abstract and they will find their object. The
Gopis meditate on the Abstract, but they find nothing in this
concept. Their love is so real that Uddhava returns to Mathura
convinced of the greatness of their love and is angry with
Krishna for ignoring Radha, Yashoda, and the Gopis.

This is the most touching of the *lilas*. The Swami weaves into
it snatches of the poetry of the Braj saint-poets. The text includes the writings of the great Surdas, Nandadas, Kumbhandas, Nigridas, and playwright Bharatendu Harishchandra of
the late nineteenth century, who lived in Banaras but wrote
Krishna songs in Braj. Raslila's chief appeal lies in its high
literary quality and its singing.

The *lila* is punctuated by tableaux that act both as climactic
points and as resting points, summing up the feeling of the
preceding scène. The tableaux, called *chhabis*, or still pictures,
relieve the monotony of song and speech and shift the aesthetic
pleasure to a different plane. They are similar in composition to
Rajput and Kangra paintings of the eighteenth and nineteenth
centuries.

The essence of Raslila is religious fervor. It binds the audience in a bond of devotion and is an acceptable release for repressed emotions and tensions, as Lord Krishna's lyrical grace
draws admiration from both men and women. Cymbals,
chanting, drums, and slogans add to the fury of the maddened
ecstasy. An important rhythm instrument is the *khartal*, a pair
of wooden clappers fitted with brass rings, which the singer
holds between the thumb and fingers of each hand. By gripping and releasing the clappers, he produces a rattling jingle
and sings and dances to its rhythm. As he plays and the tempo
quickens, he grows more and more excited. The sadhus, devotees, and worshipers often use the *khartal*.

The best Krishna is always a good singer. His acting is
stylized. The dialogue is delivered in monosyllables or half-
syllables. The Ramlila in Varanasi borrowed this style of delivery from the Raslila, which was codified much earlier.
Krishnalila, a cycle of plays on Krishna's life, was performed
in the Varanasi ghats long before Ramlila started.

The same sense of purity and detachment is observed in

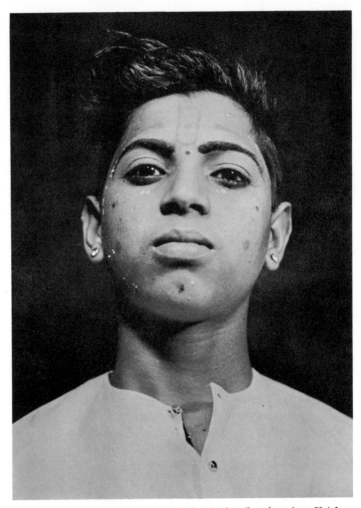

A thirteen-year-old boy from a Brahmin family who plays Krishna in a Raslila mandali

Raslila as in Ramlila. While Ramlila has the character of a pageant and is spread over a number of nights in different acting locales with multiple sets, Raslila depends solely on song and poetry, is more compact, and does not leave the temple courtyards.

Krishna, Radha, and the Gopis are always played by boys under fourteen. A boy between eleven and thirteen is the ideal Krishna. When his voice breaks, he is no longer considered fit for the role. The Gopis are played by boys of eight to ten, sometimes as young as six. Wearing colored dhotis and with heavily painted faces, they sing and dance and hop like rabbits. They are innocent, performing a ritual.

Krishna wears a *kat-kacchani* (tunic) and a peacock-feather crown. The followers of Vallabhacharya keep the peacock plume tilted to the right, while those who follow the Nimbark tradition, started by Shree Bhatt, keep it on the left. The philosophical interpretations of these two rival sects also differ. Vallabhacharya preached the worship of Krishna as a child; followers of the Nimbark path believe in the more sensuous worship of Radha and Krishna in their adult forms.

In addition to his peacock-feather crown, Krishna wears flower garlands, a colored blouse, and either a stiff skirt spreading out below the waist or a pale lemon-colored dhoti with a golden girdle. He has concentric circles of mica on his cheeks, a red flower design on his chin, and a pearl drop in his nose. Radha wears a silk *orhni* with lace and stars, a blouse, necklaces, garlands, a loose flowing skirt, and a beaded nose ring. On her cheeks and chin there are round designs in white and yellow.

Mansukh (Krishna's friend), anxious and daring and stupid, has dabs of white on his cheeks. The Samaji wears a turban, a full-sleeved *baghal bandi* (a short jacket laced with string), and a dhoti.

Krishna stealing butter

In the *ras*, the dance can be extended or curtailed according to the Swami's discretion. In between the dance sequences, while Krishna and the Gopis rest, he sings a song based on a folk melody but with a quicker rhythm.

At the Janma Ashtami festival (Krishna's birthday) in August, Krishna and the Gopis are kept in a religious atmosphere in the temple. The Swami and the musicians observe celibacy and fast for self-purification, eating only milk and fruits.

There are two important *akharas* (schools) of the Krishna-Radha faith, the Turra and the Kalagi, both found all over North India. The Turra believes in Brahma as the supreme god and its followers therefore emphasize Krishna in their worship. The Kalagi considers the goddess Shakti (Female Energy) more powerful and therefore exalts Radha.

A Raslila troupe generally consists of five musicians, the Swami, and the principal characters—Krishna and Radha, the clownish Mansukh, and six Gopis. The Swami pays the players.

Mansukh, the Clown in Raslila

Krishna's pay varies from one hundred to two hundred rupees a month. Radha and the other principal characters are paid eighty rupees a month, and the Gopis forty rupees or less. A good drummer earns sixty rupees a month, a *sarangi* player about eighty rupees. Traveling and food expenses are paid by the Swami, the leader and master of the troupe. Each musician is paid one rupee extra per performance. A good troupe earns between fifteen hundred and two thousand rupees a month.

About thirty-five professional *mandalis* are operating in Braj Bhoomi. They are invited to distant towns in Gujarat, Maharashtra, and Uttar Pradesh and are paid about five hundred rupees plus traveling expenses for each performance. Most troupes are using more and more popular folk and film tunes, but some of them preserve the old traditions. The leading *mandali* is that of Har Govind Goswami, which preserves the literary compositions and tunes of the old masters and maintains the old style.

It is customary for the rich industrialists of Ahmedabad and the wealthy houses of Delhi and Uttar Pradesh to arrange the chanting of scriptures, the *Gita* or the *Bhagavata Purana*, and conclude with a Raslila performance. When a new house is to be sanctified, or an industrialist is under legal scrutiny for black-market operations, or a son has recovered from a serious illness, these are occasions for the chanting of scriptures and a Raslila. The performance is held in the courtyard of the flower-decorated house. Incense fumes create a religious atmosphere. Women sit in silence with their heads covered and listen to the *lila*.

Theatrically, Raslila is poor. It offers the actor very little scope. It is a world of make-believe in which Krishna does not act but is taken for Krishna. Whatever he does on the stage or in the dressing room or in the passage or after the *lila* performance, he is Krishna and the people in the audience are his devotees. His acting span is hardly four years. There is no opportunity for training in a system of acting. Even the Kathak style dance and the classical melodies, essential elements in the performance, are flatly executed.

The audience is attracted by the art of the Swami, by Krishna's physical charm and singing, and by the superb literary quality of the text. Raslila *mandalis* have kept alive the great treasure of Braj literature as well as the religious and philosophical concepts of the gurus.

THERUKOOTHU

IN SOUTH India the classical and the folk theater have a stronger link. Both have the same kind of preliminaries, musical instruments, invocation songs, and both make use of a small curtain from behind which the actor reveals himself. They use towering headgear, jewelry, crowns, opulent costumes and make-up.

Tamilnad is the land of ancient temples, classical dances, palm trees, rituals, and a very ancient language. (It does not have the letters g, kh, bh, gh, or chh. "Goa" could be read as "Koa," "Delhi" as "Tilli," "Gandhi" as "Kanti.") Giant temples are dedicated to Lord Shiva, Vishnu, and other major Hindu deities. Almost every house enshrines an image of some god. Even hotels have icons placed in niches. Shiva, called Nataraja (the King of Dancers), is the great patron of actors and dancers.

In this heavily classical land the folk theater is poor. Therukoothu, which has a long tradition and a superb dramatic form, has faded into the background. The connoisseurs of Tamilnad do not give enough recognition to the folk play. They admire classical music and dance and look down upon folk drama as a rigid Brahmin might look down upon a pariah. In the slum areas of Madras there are at least fifty amateur Therukoothu troupes, but few people know of them.

Therukoothu (theru = street, koothu = play), the folk drama of Tamilnad, has existed for centuries. It is performed on a stage fourteen feet square at street level. The spectators sit on three sides. The fourth is reserved for the Pinpattu (pin = back, pattu = song, i.e., background music), which sits on a wooden divan.

The Pinpattu consists of vocalists, kurukuzhal (a small pipe resembling nagaswaram), maddalam (drum), and talam (small cymbals). Nowadays a harmonium is used to serve as drone in place of bagpipes, which used to be in vogue. In the old days metal cymbals were selected according to the singer's voice, which was always high-pitched. The cymbals gave the beat as well as the pitch, a combination of rhythm and tone.

The play opens with the worship of Ganesha. An actor wearing an elephant-head mask dances while the musicians sing an invocation song. After the dance he sits on a small wooden bench and is worshiped by a priest. Then the chorus invokes Shiva, Meenakshi, Dakshinamurthi (one of Shiva's forms who always sits facing south), Saraswati (Goddess of Learning), and finally Trimurthi (Brahma, Vishnu, and Shiva).

After this brief introduction, the Kattiakaran (Stage Manager) sings from behind a curtain held by two stagehands. He comes forward and describes himself in the third person. He wears a gold headdress, necklaces, bracelets, and a flowing tunic with a sword tucked into a silken girdle. He announces the play, comments on it, and links up the scenes. In *Meenakshi Ammai Natakam* ("The Drama of Goddess Meenakshi"), one of the earliest published plays,* the Kattiakaran announces the arrival of the king in a song. Then he addresses the orchestra in prose: "Maddala-karan! Tithi-karan! Talam-karan! Let your orchestra be perfect. Don't play out of tune! The king is coming. Don't play too fast. Don't make mistakes in the beat. Who is making that noise? Shut up! If you speak I shall thrash you. No noise!"

After this scolding in prose, he sings the glory of the king. The king announces himself in the third person in a song: "The Pandya king has come! The king whose name is Malayadhavaja has come!"

Every composition in Karnatak music has three parts: *pallavi, anu-pallavi,* and *charanam*—the beginning, the middle, and the end.

After the king has sung *pallavi* he sings *anu-pallavi,* describing his position, kingdom, and glory: "The king who rules Madura, the ever-fertile land, the king whose fame has no bounds. He comes!" He goes on: "The golden crown glitters on his head. He wears large rings in his ears, majestic decorations on his shoulders, ruby-studded necklaces on his chest, and holds the scepter in his hand. With the name of Lord Shiva in his heart, he comes! The Pandya king comes!" He talks to the Kattiakaran. "Listen, our palace guard! I want to have some fun now. Bring the performers, dancers, and wrestlers!"

The Kattiakaran shouts: "Who is there? The dancing master? Come! The king wants all of you. Where are your dancing girls? Bring them!"

Dancers, musicians, wrestlers, and ministers come. The queen enters. They announce themselves, describing their appearance, deeds, parentage, achievements, and glory.

The Komali (Buffoon) always makes a startling entry. He may jump from a tree or a housetop, or roll down a haystack. He enters slapping and beating the spectators with a cloth whip, stumbling and jumping over their heads. He announces himself with a song in the third person, changes to prose, and makes fun of the highest and the noblest.

In *Lava Kusha Natakam* the Komali is known as Asthana Santoshi (the man who is pleased with people). He enters with these words: "Here comes Asthana, an easy-going chap, blessing everyone he meets. He claims to be the king's com-

---

* *Meenakshi Ammai Natakam,* edited and corrected by Tyagaraja Pillai, Astrologer-Pundit (Tamilnad: Tiruchi Bookshops, 1889).

mander-in-chief. He can cut a tender pumpkin in two with one stroke of his sword. He can predict that soft leaves sprout from a forest plant. He knows the scientific truth that hemlock is a bitter herb. Still people call him a worthless fellow! Anyway he has come now."

He addresses the audience in a chant. "Why are you shouting? Why are you unruly? Why do you run to occupy seats in one direction like pigs jumping in a pond? Keep peace. Silence! Watch the play and go home with your heart full of joy!" Then he sings, "Why do you shout for actors? You had a good dinner. You've chewed betel. Why do you shout? Sit quietly and watch the spectacle on the stage. Here comes Rama, King of Ayodhya. Bow to him. Rama is coming flanked by his brothers and followed by Sita. . . ."

He describes the status of the characters, their costumes, actions, and feelings. Thus the Komali does the job of the Kattiakaran in the opening scene. When the Kattiakaran takes over, the Komali tries to baffle him with questions, contradictions, riddles, and mockery. This exchange brings out the theme and purpose of the play.

In most traditional dance-dramas, characters are introduced from behind a hand-held curtain. In Yakshagana, Kuchipudi, Kathakali, and Bhagavatha Mela, the entries of main characters are always full of suspense. The actor treats the curtain as a stage property, peering and grimacing over it, clutching it, and dancing behind it. He establishes his character by his entry. The haughty demons and power-drunk titans are spellbinding as they grunt and stomp, giving partial glimpses to the audience.

While most dance-dramas have richly embroidered silk curtains, the Therukoothu uses a length of white cotton cloth (thirai cheelai). The face and feet of the character are visible as the curtain conceals him from chin to knees. He dances and sings and explains his entry in a song. This introduction is in the third person, giving an element of abstraction, a sense of detachment as if another man were speaking for the characters. The song fits the temperament of the character. This convention of self-introduction is observed in many Eastern theaters. In the Peking Opera the actor introduces himself in the first person. So do the characters in a Kabuki play. But the Therukoothu character describes himself in the third person, talks in the first person when he converses with other characters, then slips back to third person. This gives the character a double perspective, revealing his mind at two levels. He is his own critic.

Because of Therukoothu's vigorous character, all roles are played by men. Every character enters according to his temperament: tame, furious, haughty. Each treats the Kattiakaran according to his position, some kindly, some angrily, some indifferently. The Kattiakaran repeats the character's main words, adding tempo and clarity to the dialogue. The characters dance with simple steps, cut capers, tumble, and do acrobatics. Wriggling their shoulders, they go around the arena like triumphant gladiators. After a dance sequence, the characters rest while the Kattiakaran entertains the audience with a song.

Therukoothu is essentially operatic; only about 10 per cent of it is in prose, supplemented with impromptu dialogue and the repetitive questions of the Komali and the Kattiakaran. Some songs are verses without rhythmic beats, half chanting, half singing, like the *alaap* of a classical melody. (The *alaap* in an introductory elaboration of the notes of a melody, sung without words to bring out the features of the *raga*. It is always done in slow motion, like the rising of smoke.)

The chanting (*virutham*) precedes every song in Therukoothu. It always contains four lines. The length of the lines varies; it may have six, eight, or sixteen syllables. The *virutham* is usually set in the same *raga* as the song and leads to the next situation in the play. The singer chants the words to underline the meaning, sums up the situation, and makes the audience understand clearly the progress of the story. This breaks the monotony of the singing.

Either the chorus or the actor himself sings the *virutham*. The singer can interrupt it at any moment, go back to the first line, halt, spin the word into a short musical aria, and then proceed. The *talam* and *maddalam* players join the singing chorus. Every character knows all the songs by heart.

Themes are drawn mostly from the epics, the *Puranas*, and folktales. The most popular plays are based on the *Mahabharata*. A Therukoothu repertoire is inconceivable without the haughty Duryodhana, the vicious Dushasana, the noble Dharma, the proud Keechaka, the mighty Bhima. Draupadi, the common wife of the five Pandava brothers in the *Mahabharata* epic, is the pivotal heroine. When the eldest brother stakes everything in a game of dice and loses his kingdom, his brothers, himself, and even Draupadi to the Kauravas, Draupadi is dragged into the court of Duryodhana by his brother Dushasana. Krishna's timely intervention saves her from being stripped naked. Most of the plays of vengeance, blood, irony, and honor revolve around this insult. Draupadi vows to let her hair fall loose until she shall dip it into Duryodhana's blood.

In Tamilnad, Draupadi has been deified. A cycle of eight plays is performed in her honor every year. These eight dramas of blood and vengeance are played with ferocious grandeur before Draupadi's temple on consecutive nights. On the ninth day Bhima, the strongest of the Pandava brothers, smashes Duryodhana's thigh and avenges Draupadi's honor. She smears her hair with Duryodhana's blood and ties it up. This drama is performed in the morning in a terrifyingly realistic way. A clay effigy of Duryodhana sprawls on the ground before the temple. Bhima smashes his thigh with his mace. The clay figure breaks and squirts blood-red liquid. Bhima grunts exultantly and becomes revenge incarnate. The finale is the worship of Draupadi, which takes the form of a solemn ritual.

The best known Raghava Thambiran troupe is led by Sri Natesa Thambiran of Purisai village, who belongs to a family of traditional Therukoothu actors. Natesa specializes in the role of Dushasana. Some years ago he used to announce his entry with an explosion. Holding a stick loaded with gunpowder, he danced and sang behind the curtain before he made his furious entry. During one performance the explosion blew off his left hand and two fingers of his right hand. Today, even with a missing hand, he is the best actor of this type. His eyes spit fire when he drags Draupadi into the court of Duryodhana.

In Therukoothu, as in Kathakali and Bhagavatha Mela, extremely imaginative acting is mixed with devilishly realistic episodes such as the pulling out of Keechaka's entrails by Bhima or the tearing of the demon king Hiranyakashipu's belly by Narasimha. Here is scope for uncontrolled emotion. The

Dushasana (Sri Natesa Thambiran) stripping Draupadi in the court of the Kauravas

words are made more powerful by drumming. In *Prahlada Charitram*, the lion-headed Narasimha sometimes goes into a trance. Cases have been known of physical violence committed by actors portraying Narasimha or Bhima.

Another popular play is *Vallikalyanam* ("The Marriage of the Goddess Valli"). Valli is found as a child in a field that has just been harvested. A hunter-king brings her up. She is asked to guard over a crop lest the birds destroy it. Lord Subramania, son of Shiva, also known as Murugan, has heard of Valli's beauty and comes to the field disguised as a hunter. As he is talking to her the king's sons come upon them. Subramania assumes the form of a tree, then of a bangle-seller, before he finally reveals his real form and marries Valli. Subramania, a powerful god of Tamilnad, is worshiped in almost every home, and his name is a popular one. In the Central Secretariat in New Delhi there are easily a hundred Subramaniams, ranging from a minister to a section officer.

Meenakshi Ammai Natakam also has an interesting story. The king and queen of Madurai are childless. They perform a yagna. The goddess Parvati, Shiva's spouse, appears as a three-year-old baby and is named Meenakshi. She is a peculiar divine child with three breasts. A heavenly voice announces that her third breast will disappear when she meets her future consort, and that she will be the future queen of Madurai. She learns swordplay and archery. After the king's death, she becomes the queen and sets out to conquer Mount Kailasa, where Lord Shiva lives. Shiva comes to Madurai in the human form of Sundareswara and marries her.

After their marriage the yogis and saints request Lord Shiva to dance the same celestial dance that he had danced at Chidambaram, in which his left foot was lifted. He dances, but with one difference. This time he lifts his right foot. After the dance the king and queen rule the country. In the end they enter the temple and disappear. From then on the temple is worshiped as Meenakshi Sundareswara Temple.

MAKE-UP

Therukoothu, with its gilded crowns and heavy make-up, has a family resemblance to Kathakali. But it does not have the artistic splendor of the classical form.

Epic heroes like Duryodhana, Dharma, Bhima, and Hiranyakashipu wear tall crowns decorated with bits of colored mirror. This headgear, made of the light wood punna, is an arched bracket with a pinnacled dome embellished with green, red, and gold patterns. The massive shoulder decorations look like the clipped wings of a bird. Red and black crescents are drawn above the heavily shaded eyes of the characters. A silver band is scrawled across the forehead. Ornaments, chest decorations, armbands, and bracelets are crusted with shining specks.

Villains are painted red with white and black dots. Bhima wears blue and black make-up; Krishna wears translucent green; Narasimha wears a lion-head mask. Every character is fitted with ankle bells and is required to dance.

Dushasana has a black beard, three white lines on his forehead, a glistening mustache made of black wool mixed with
wax, and white and red dots on his face. He wears a round
golden cap with red and green designs, tight-fitting trousers,
bells around his ankles, and a billowy tunic.

The priest wears large earrings (kundalam), three stripes
of sandalwood paste on his forehead, a garland of rudra beads
(rudrakshmala), a white silk dhoti, and the sacred thread
across his chest. On one finger of the right hand he wears a
ring of holy grass. He brings a pot of water, flowers, and incense and recites Sanskrit shlokas in praise of the god Ganesha.

The Komali has a conical cap, white bellows-shaped
trousers (sometimes a dhoti is draped in this style), a U-shaped
mark on his forehead, a pot belly, a flowing beard made of
white manji fiber, thick eyebrows, and red and black spots all
over his face.*

The Komali is the darling of the spectators. In antholog-
ical plays, he shocks the audience out of the old world and
brings them face to face with contemporary life. He will say:
"I want to ask a boon from Shiva. My wife has been pregnant
for thirteen months. There is nobody in the house to fetch
water. Please, Shiva, come and help her!" Highest respect is
shown to sages and yogis, but the Komali can make fun of
them. He is free, gay, uninhibited; he can poke fun at life and
even mock at death.

The Kattiakaran, who manages the stage, is present throughout. He alternates between dignified humility and brash ar-
rogance. His use of prose and song and the mixture of chaste
Tamil and local dialect are brilliant. He controls the rhythm
of the play. The Komali fills it with laughter. He must have
ready wit, be a superb improviser, and make the task of Kattiakaran easy. His speech is rustic. He puts questions to the
characters, draws them out, and makes them repeat their lines.
Like peasants bargaining at a fair, the characters repeat their
words so often that the unwary, the inattentive, even the deaf
will understand. At times it becomes almost boring. In Bhima
Jatasuran Sandai ("The Battle of Bhima and Jatasuran"), the
sage is worried.

Chorus (sings): O Sage, what is your real worry?
Kattiakaran: Do you know what they are asking?
Sage: What?
Komali: They are asking what is your worry?
Sage: My worry is . . .
Komali: Tell them why you are worried.

* This is the Komali's make-up in a nineteenth-century folk song.

Another scene from the play The Stripping of Draupadi *performed*
by the troupe of Sri Natesa Thambiran

The dialogue is repeated three times. The character sings; the chorus repeats; the actor comes forward and talks to the Kattiakaran or the Komali in prose in order to be more easily understood.

There are many styles of folk *natakas* (plays). Nondi Natakam (lame play), also called Orrukal Natakam (one-legged play), is a solo performance. The actor ties one leg so that his foot touches his buttocks. He says that his leg has been lost in the king's battle. He seeks people's sympathy. Narrating his story (he plays many characters) with exaggerated gestures, he moves the people to pity. His art can be compared with that of a dissembling beggar who pretends to be a blind man, a leper, or a paralytic and tells his woeful tale to passers-by in order to collect money. Nondi Natakam has a robust misery, drawing both tears and laughter. The art demands great concentration.

Pagal Vesham is performed in the daytime by a two-man troupe. They may impersonate a thief and a police chief, a haughty teacher and a lazy pupil, an old husband and a young wife, a moneylender and a poor client. If they perform the thief and police chief in one part of the city, the following day they will play the same piece in another area. Masters of make-up and verisimilitude, they portray scenes from life. A cruel husband spurns his wife in the street, threatening to leave her. The wife begs him to pardon her. He flares up and beats her. A crowd gathers. The people try to persuade the husband to pardon the miserable wife. The husband rebukes the crowd, kicks his wife, and leaves her behind wailing and sobbing. Believing this to be a true event, the people take pity and help the wife with money. She gets up, ties the money in a fold of her sari, and laughs slyly. She is a Pagal Vesham actor. Husband and wife bow to the public and receive more money in appreciation of their art.

Pagal Vesham is on the decline. It has been reduced to fancy dress for such occasions as the Pongal festival, Deepavali, and Dashahara.

In Madras city slum areas there are at least fifty small amateur Therukoothu troupes, but they are little known. They perform to small audiences of the poor folk amidst thatched huts and oil lamps. Every player contributes a small sum to the troupe, the heroine and hero paying more than the others. This goes to defray the expenses of production and to pay the Kattiakaran, who teaches them for two or three months before they stage the play.

The actors are farmers, laborers, fishermen, watchmen, coolies. Fifteen to twenty actors make an ensemble. Their theater is not demonstrative. They perform to please themselves. A command performance can be arranged for one hundred rupees. Most of the money goes toward the costs of production: gaslight, the hire of costumes, make-up, and an offering to the guru.

The most famous Therukoothu troupes have come from the southern districts of Tamilnad, areas contiguous to Kerala, and have apparently been influenced by Kathakali. Except for Natesa Thambiran, the players are stiff, cold, inexperienced. They do not have the abandon and inner harmony necessary in folk singing, folk dancing, and folk acting. Therukoothu as a dramatic form is far more interesting than is apparent in actual performances today. It has power in its operatic songs, and reveals theatrical shrewdness in the character of Kattiakaran and his function.

Chapter Nine

YAKSHAGANA

IN SOUTH India between Kerala and Maharashtra lies Karnatak. Its west coast strip has the gorgeous folk theater, Yakshagana, which means music of the heavenly Yakshas.

Yakshagana, an operatic dance-drama, is over three hundred years old. Its temperament is *tandava*, full of valor and anger and terror. Its songs—literary compositions set to a distinct type of music—were sung and danced in temple courtyards and village squares. Slowly the form took the name of the style of musical composition.

The themes are taken from the *Ramayana, the Mahabharata*, and the *Puranas*. Mythological heroes, gods, and demons people the stage. All the plays have battle scenes, even those dealing with marriage and diplomatic missions. *Girja Kalyana* ("Marriage of Girja") opens with a fierce battle between Shiva and Daksha. In *Subhadra Kalyana* ("Marriage of Subhadra") the valiant Arjuna fights Subhadra's cousins and brothers. The words and musical compositions are set to bring out the heroic. Almost all the important battles in the *Mahabharata* and the *Ramayana* have been exploited in the Yakshagana repertoire.

The coastal belt of Karnatak—including North and South Kanara—is full of spice gardens, cashew nut estates, feathery palms, and paddy fields. The beaches are washed by roaring waves. Rivers shoot down from the hills into the sea. In this natural setting, Yakshagana expresses the energetic spirit of the landscape. Its towering headgears, high-pitched singing, wild drumming, and vigorous dancing offer the rare feast of a dance-opera of the traditional type.

North Kanara preserves the more individualized and pure form of Yakshagana.

The performance is held in a village square, on a sandy beach, or in a field. About a dozen professional troupes tour this coastal land. It is difficult to know in advance where the show is to be. The troupes are constantly on the move. They travel in a bullock cart or a lorry, or they cross water inlets by ferries. To find the best troupe one has to search for it over waterlogged fields.

PRELIMINARIES AND PERFORMANCE

A Yakshagana play starts at nine in the evening and lasts all night. The stage is sixteen feet square and at ground level. A pole is fixed in each of the four corners with plantains tied to them. Their large leaves sway and bend and meet high up in the air, forming a feathery canopy. Two waist-high metal lamps brimming with coconut oil sputter and blaze. The audience sits on three sides.

The Bhagavatha (Director and Singing Chorus) sits up-

A Yakshagana performance goes on throughout the night

stage, holding tiny cymbals. He is accompanied by three instrumentalists: one plays on the *maddale* (drum), one on a
pipe, one on the *chande* (a barrel-like drum with a sharp clattering sound, particularly effective in battle scenes).

The image of Ganesha is worshiped by the actors in the
dressing room, where it remains throughout the night. After
the make-up is complete, the actor bows before Ganesha,
chants *mantras*, closes his eyes, meditates, and walks to the
stage as if hypnotized. The opening song by the Bhagavatha
is also in praise of Ganesha. Two men hold a small, brightly
embroidered curtain. Either the figure of Ganesha or its head

is revealed from behind the curtain, or ornaments and crowns are shown. Ganesha is never impersonated. He is not a character; he is the deity, to be worshiped.

After the prayer the Hanumanayaka (Buffoon) enters. He plays the announcer, the messenger, the servant—anything. He puts questions to each incoming character and draws him out. His remarks are disrespectful and meaningful.

Hanumanayaka: Having saluted the lords of Eight Directions, now I am asking who is more prominent—the god or the king? Well, God. Which god? God of the Earth, which means my king.

The Bhagavatha sings in praise of the audience. This is followed by a prose bit, which fades into a *shloka* eulogizing the king. The Bhagavatha and Hanumanayaka quote ancient scriptures, linking their folk tradition with the classical:

Hanumanayaka (prose): What are the elements of a good audience?

Bhagavatha (verse): The scholar, the poet, the eulogizer, the musician, the clown, the historian, and the man well versed in legends. These are the seven constituents of a good audience.

Hanumanayaka: What should be the seating arrangement?

Bhagavatha (*Sanskrit shloka*): To the left the drummers, a little behind them the cymbalist, between them the singer, to his side the eulogizer, to his left the clown, in front of them the dancers.

Hanumanayaka: And the stage dimensions?

Bhagavatha (*shloka*): Five *hastas* [cubits] by ten *hastas*, shaped like the half moon.*

Hanumanayaka: On such a stage, what should be the characteristics of a Bhagavatha?

Bhagavatha: "Bha" means the devotee of Bhagawan [Lord], "Ga" means devoid of *garva* [pride], "Va" means profound in *vakya* [speech], "Tha" stands for *tattva-nirnaya* [sound in judgment].

Hanumanayaka: The shape of the drum?

Bhagavatha (*shloka*): The drum should be made of dry wood, round in shape with a bulge in the middle. The two ends should be like the sun and the moon.

Hanumanayaka: How to achieve the emotion?

Bhagavatha (*shloka*): Where the hand goes, there the eyes; where the eyes go, there the mind; where the mind goes, there the emotion!

* Though the Yakshagana stage is square, the Bhagavatha quotes a *shloka* to give his statement sanctity.

After a long conversation describing the stage conventions *
and aesthetic principles, the two characters break the serious
mood:

Hanumanayaka: O, noise! Noise!

Bhagavatha: All right, make enough noise!

Hanumanayaka: Aha, Bhagavatha! In this arena where we are
to stage the play, who is that looking almost like a mountain?

Bhagavatha: Fool, don't talk blasphemy. The god Vinayaka
is present here to bless the Bhagavatha, the audience, the
devotees—everyone who seeks his help.

Hanumanayaka: Is it true?

Bhagavatha: True.

Hanumanayaka: Repeat it three times.

Bhagavatha: Yes, three times.

Hanumanayaka: He helps everyone who seeks his help.

Bhagavatha: Yes.

Hanumanayaka: In that case I am short of money. I have to
pay a government tax. Let the god bring a bag containing
silver coins to the extent of—say five hundred times four
rupees!

Bhagavatha: It is possible if you mortgage four times that
much money.

Hanumanayaka: If I had that much money why should I come
here to perform the role of a clown?

This repartee is followed by a song in honor of Lord Shan-
mukha (the six-headed god), son of Shiva.

The Bhagavatha chants rhythmic prose salutations to the
audience and the presiding deity. Two boys, representing Bal-
arama and Krishna, enter and dance briskly. At peak points
they jump high, whirl, and in a delirious frenzy caper around
on their knees as the audience whistles and cheers. These
dancers are aspiring lads who are learning the art and perfect
it on the stage. They give the audience a foretaste of the
splendid art of the main characters.

After their exit, the Bhagavatha sings. His assistant (San-
geetkar) helps to continue the alaap (elaboration of pure
melody) and sometimes sings solo to give respite to the
Bhagavatha. But it is always the Bhagavatha alone who sings
and speaks to the characters. He also pronounces the rhythmic
syllables of the drum to emphasize the footwork.

Two women (boys in female roles) enter and dance. They
are supposed to be Satyabhama and Rukmini, Lord Krishna's

* The earliest text of Yakshagana stage conventions and preliminaries
is *Sabha Gadya* (1621). Its palm-leaf manuscript is with Shivaram
Karanth of Puttur who found it in Shimoga District.

An actor jumps high during the dance

two constantly jealous wives. The Bhagavatha sings in praise
of Lord Krishna and combines drum *bols* (rhythmic syllables)
with his song, alternating between the musical and the rhythmic. The two women display expert footwork. Suddenly they
begin doing acrobatic hops, losing themselves in energetic
dancing and replacing feminine delicacy with masculine vigor.
The furious hops are followed by hip wriggling, and the
dancers once more take up delicate feminine rhythms.

After this, the play starts with the king's court (Oddolaga)
or some opulent majestic show. This grand opening is an
occasion for dance, acrobatics, and pomp, and gives the dancer-
actor a chance to show his art.

If it is a play about the Pandavas, the five brothers are introduced one by one from behind the traditional small curtain held by two stagehands. The eldest Pandava, Yudhishtra,
enters, stands with his back toward the audience, dances,
shows his side pose, then a bit of his face, finally full face, and
vanishes. All the brothers come in one by one and then disappear. Finally they all enter with their faces toward the
spectators. Their large, glittering headgears and impressive
faces are revealed from behind the curtain. They dance a few
steps. Then the curtain is whisked to one side, and they appear
in full splendor.

In the beginning of the play, no woman accompanies the
hero. Queen Draupadi is not permitted by tradition to appear
at the first entry of the five Pandavas. If it is a *Ramayana* episode, Sita does not accompany Rama and Lakshmana.
Women are given second position in order to emphasize the
male temperament of Yakshagana.

All important characters enter first from behind the traditional colored curtain held by two stagehands. The actor bows
to the stage, touches the feet of the Bhagavatha, and does an
acrobatic dance with his back toward the audience before he
reveals his identity.

The dancer carries an arrow and a bow. The bow is always a
straight staff. He twirls it, wields it, rests against it. It gives him
a stance, a pose, a dignity. A curved bow would restrict action,
but the straight one gives strength. The actor holds this theatrical bow at arm's length with one end on the ground touching
his toe and his knee resting against it.

The characters talk in stylized speech, and each one helps
the conversation by repeating the last word of the other in a
sort of carry-forward. When one character speaks a long mono-
logue, it is broken by another with "aha," "aho," and "hao,"
expressing affirmation. Sometimes the Bhagavatha converses
with the newcomer and helps unfold his identity. If the queen
is accompanied by her maids, they add exclamatory words.

An actor in the process of make-up. He has outlined his eyes, drawn
conch-shell designs near them, fixed a sacred mark on his forehead,
and painted his jowls black

In *Subahu Kalaga* ("The Battle Fought by Subahu") Rama
has announced the horse sacrifice *yagna*. His horse has been
challenged by a demon Vidyunmali. Pushkala (Bharata's
son) gets ready for battle. He enters his palace to take leave
of his wife and says to her: "I have prepared for the battle. I am
going. I shall defeat the enemy and bring you war trophies.

Don't be sad. My armor shines, and my arrows and bow are
quivering. I shall return victorious."

This short speech will be spoken on the stage as follows:

Pushkala: I have prepared for the battle.
Wife: Aho.
Pushkala: I am going.
Wife: Where?
Pushkala: I shall defeat the enemy.
Wife: Hao!
Pushkala: And bring you war trophies.
Wife: So?
Pushkala: Don't be sad.
Wife: No.
Pushkala: My armor shines.
Wife: Aho.
Pushkala: And my arrows and bow are quivering.
Wife: Yes.
Pushkala: I shall return victorious.
Wife: No doubt!

An actor in partial make-up. The numerous long cords are used
for tying the huge turban (mundasu)

All night the stage is dominated by mythological titans, gods, ogres, superhuman heroes and heroines. Large turbans whirl like many suns. Amidst battles, war cries, acrobatic dancing, and wild drumming, the Bhagavatha sings the events vividly. When the sun's rays peep through the feathery palms, the Bhagavatha sings the *antima* (concluding song) and the actors take the big oil lamps and walk to the make-up enclosure to offer a final song in Ganesha's honor.

MAKE-UP AND COSTUMES

Fifty yards away from the acting area is an open-air enclosure fenced with palm leaves and straw mats. Crowns, girdles, ankle bells, tunics, blouses, jackets, and gilded jewelry hang on horizontal bamboo poles. Here the actors are busy putting on make-up. Except for two or three main characters, each actor plays many roles so that the "dressing room" bustles

Yakshagana actors putting on their make-up in the open-air dressing room

with activity all night. Before they start applying their make-up, the actors worship the ornaments, break a coconut, and offer it to the god Ganesha, in front of whose image a coconut oil lamp is constantly burning. Flowers, sweets, and fruits are offered to the image. Actors bow before the deity, take up the glow of the light with their hands and pass it to their eyes, and squat on the floor to put on their make-up. It is fascinating to watch them sitting cross-legged in two rows facing each other, busy with their colorful transformation.

The Yakshagana *mundasu*, a giant turban with golden ribbons radiating from the center, is the most opulent and complicated headgear. The actor ties the *mundasu* to the tuft of his hair, which he wears long for this purpose, building it up coil after coil. When it is one foot high and his hand can no longer reach the top, the make-up man helps. After every coil the turban is tightened with threads and cords. More than three hundred yards of ribbons, colored strings, and silver bands are used to fix it. The finished form is that of a huge lotus leaf with golden shafts. The more majestic the king, the larger the *mundasu*. Keechaka's headgear weighs about twelve pounds. The medieval chiefs and rajahs measured their importance by the size of their turbans. The former rulers of princely states in India mostly wore fantastically large turbans. The Yakshagana *mundasu* is a blown-up version of these.

The hero puts a U-shaped mark on his forehead with a red flame in the center, a white conch-shell design above his nose between his eyebrows, and conch-shell designs on the left and right corners of his eyes. These white designs are picked out by a fine red outline. His jet-black mustache, made of thickly matted cotton threads, runs across his cheeks and down his ears and is tied at the back in a knot. His beard is not on his face but starts from his chin and moves along his jowls on both sides in two black-painted sectors.* This leaves space for the flat ink-black mustache, making it vivid and strong, a symbol of male prowess.

A green, red, or black jacket fits the actor's torso. The thickly spun nine-yard checkered dhoti is folded double and tied so that a pleated length hangs down in front. A white or red silken scarf flutters down the back of the *mundasu* and is tucked up in the girdle. A red-lined white cloth goes around the neck, crosses over the breast and is knotted at the back, and hangs down behind like a fluttering tail.

* This form of beard appears in earlier paintings of the Malanad area. The Gudigar artisans of Karnatak carved figures with beards like this on temple chariots. The twelfth-century Muslim Pashas also had such beards. The Kanara coastal people had close connections with the Arabs and Abyssinians during the ninth and tenth centuries.

A Yakshagana Demon partly made up

The leading characters wear *kernappo* (ear decorations), *kordahara* (chest adornment), *soge* (necklace), *tolapavada* (bracelets), *bhujakeerti* (epaulettes), *dagale* (red and gold beaded girdle), and anklets. All the ornaments except the anklets are fashioned of gilded wood. The headgear, costumes, and jewelry are heavy. Ravana's full costume may weigh twenty pounds.

When the actor enters the arena in his dazzling make-up, the *chande* clatters and gives him added ferocity. Despite his massive headgear and heavy costume, he dances, jumps, and kicks with lightning speed. The moment he exits he is a different being. Perspiring and panting, he sprawls on the mats behind the instrumentalists. He cannot take off his *mundasu* because it is tied with complicated knots. He may sleep until his next cue.

In *Subahu Kalaga*, a favorite play, the sixty-one-year-old Harady Rama plays the youthful Pushkala. The make-up transforms him. He jumps, roars, and dances. It is difficult to believe that behind the gilded *mundasu* and jet-black mustache of the valiant Pushkala is a balding, wrinkled old man.

Duryodhana, Yudhishtra, Krishna, Rama, Lakshmana, Bharata, Shatrughna, and all emperors wear *kireetas* (crowns) of gold and silver. The *kireeta* is flanked by two swans with red flowers in their beaks; a silver lotus is embossed on the upper part; peacock feathers adorn the top. The minister is dressed in a tunic, a small puggree, and a dhoti, and holds a staff. The Bhagavatha wears a white shirt, white dhoti, and red turban. Women wear necklaces, golden girdles studded with bits of glass, bracelets, and leaf-shaped crimson pads with silver stripes at the backs of their heads. They generally wear a black cotton sari nine yards long with a vermilion border. The blouse is red for contrast.

The make-up of Surpanakha (Ravana's sister) gives her an awesome appearance. She wears a peacock-feather crown, its tassels swaying high. Red and white half moons are painted on her forehead, white dots on her cheeks, and red lines below her eyes. Long jute fibers hang down from her head. She wears multicolored large skirts. Her hips are padded and thrust back in an ugly bulge. A white perforated bib frames her cheeks and chin. As she bellows, the white strips of the bib flap. She changes her costume in view of the audience when she wants to become Maya Surpanakha, the Illusion, who goes out to avenge the wrong done to her by Rama and Lakshmana.

The hunter wears a *kore-mundasu* (tilted turban) which covers almost half of one cheek.

A hero affixes his long black mustache

THE BHAGAVATHA

The success of a Yakshagana depends chiefly on the art of the Bhagavatha. Throughout the performance he sings for the characters, commenting on their actions, linking up events. The characters speak out extempore in prose what the Bhagavatha sings. He starts at a high pitch and raises his voice as if he were loudly calling, challenging, wailing. His high-crested voice constructs a many-pinnacled fortress. He breaks the words and makes their outline clear. The notes of the song do not fade. They suddenly stop in the middle as if a high tree were cut with one stroke of a hatchet. The singing has a majesty, a rugged untamed grandeur.

The songs are set in *talas* with punctuation to allow dancing. The music is of a special variety, falling somewhere between the folk and the classical. Many ragas used in Yakshagana are not found either in Hindustani or in Karnatak music. Old Yakshagana plays mention about 150 ragas of which 30 are rare compositions. Some of the melodies found exclusively in Yakshagana are tujavantoo, panchagati, ghantarawa, huvu, mechhu, davalara, and many others.

The Bhagavatha, while narrating an event, speaks in the third person. Generally the narrative uses a literary poetical structure. It can be a kanda, a four-line metrical form of Sanskrit prosody, or a vrita, with a somewhat longer structure. Neither of these forms is meant to be sung or danced as they do not divide equally in relation to time beats. They are used in Yakshagana primarily for narration. The poetical forms employed by the Bhagavatha are dwipadi (couplets), tripadi (three lines), chaupadi (four lines), and shatpadi (six lines). In dwipadi and chaupadi the end words rhyme. Some of the shatpadis are sung to talas.

The actors sit cross-legged doing their make-up

The Bhagavatha comments on the action and tells the inner thoughts of the characters. He acts as the detached observer, the reporter, the commentator, and at times sings on behalf of the character, identifying himself completely with the role. In a scene in *Lava-Kushara Kalaga* ("Battle Fought by Lava and Kusha"), Sita sees her son Lava returning to the hermitage alone and asks him where her other son is. Lava tells her that he has sent his brother against his will to help a needy woman in the forest. Hearing this, Sita's heart sinks.

At this point the Bhagavatha sings what she is thinking: "My sons went together to the forest, but only one has returned. It reminds me of my own state of affairs." The audience understands the "state of affairs" she is referring to. Much earlier, when she was in exile with Rama, she sent Lakshmana away from the hut much against his will. Left alone, she was carried away by Ravana. She is reminded of her past and is thinking of the calamity that may have befallen her son in the forest. The audience understands and relates Sita's past with the present. At such moments the emotional impact is strong. It is the situation, the silence of Sita, and the words of the Bhagavatha's song that conjure up the past and bring the spectators to an awareness of the awful reality.

Gopalakrishna Kamath is a lovely-voiced Bhagavatha, evocative, charged with emotion. His singing lends a lusty color to the play. He belongs to the Mandarthi Mela.

The earliest extant palm-leaf manuscript of a Yakshagana play appears to be *Virata Parva* (1564), an episode from the *Mahabharata* written by Vishnu Varamballi. The poet Devidasa from Barkur village wrote many Yakshaganas, of which ten are available in print. *Krishnarjunara Kalaga* ("Krishna-Arjuna Battle," 1680), *Abhimanyu Kalaga* ("The Battle Fought by Abhimanyu"), *Saindhava Vadh* ("Murder of Saindhava") are a part of the popular repertoire throughout Karnatak. An unknown devotee wrote eight *Ramayana* plays, the earliest of which is *Putra Kameshti* ("Dasaratha's Penance for Begetting a Son," 1652). Rama Bhatta, a prolific writer and composer, left behind *Subhadra Kalyana* ("Marriage of Subhadra") and *Lava-Kushara Kalaga*.

Early in this century Yakshagana was taught along with arithmetic in the village schools. The children learned music, poetry, local myths, lore, and tradition through Yakshagana. During Dashahara days the teacher took his band of pupils holding flower wands and visited households in the village streets. They sang *chaupadis*, requesting the host to bless their teacher with gifts. Then they would act out a scene. Even today funds are sometimes raised in villages by the Bhagavatha and his students in the old manner.

Harady Rama as the hero Pushkala in Subahu Kalaga

Modern critics, influenced by the realistic drama of the nineteenth century, have ignored the literary merits of these traditional song-dramas. Yet *Iravatha* ("Tale of the Celestial Elephant"), and Nagappayya's *Chandravali*, both of the seventeenth century, have superb literary and dramatic qualities.

Yakshagana is not folk art in the sense of being spontaneous expression. It is a self-conscious, highly developed operatic form that demands perfect knowledge of classical music, *talas*, epics, and ancient plays. Its rigid classical singing, intricate footwork, and quotations from Sanskrit texts make it a bit removed from the folk. But the virile dancing, tumbling, acrobatics, extemporaneous speech, and the absence of a strict *abhinaya* language give it a folk character.

In North Kanara about a dozen *melas* (troupes) tour the villages. They are named after a temple or a village. Mandarthi Mela takes its name from a village where the goddess Bhagavathi is the chief deity, Amriteshwari Mela from the goddess Amriteshwari, and Kollur Mela, Maranakatte Mela, and Indugunji Mela from villages with particular religious backgrounds. A *mela* generally consists of twenty people: dancers, singers, actors, musicians, stagehands. For six months, from November 15 to May 15, they perform every night for twelve hours. As the east starts graying and the rays of the sun begin to redden the sky, the play comes to an end. The players pack their costumes and ornaments in large straw boxes and set out for the next town. They eat a hurried meal of rice and hot spiced curry, sleep through the afternoon, and then get ready for the next performance. When the monsoons start, every open-air cultural activity comes to an end. After the monsoons, the air is clean and the land is bursting with greenery. This is the season of dance-dramas, pageants, and festivals.

TALA MADDALE

The coastal people have evolved an indoor form, Tala Maddale or Prasanga, which follows the Yakshagana repertoire and rules but does not use costumes, make-up, or dance. The Bhagavatha sits on the floor along with the drummers. The artists sit in two rows opposite each other. They are called Arthadhari (those who expound the meaning) as contrasted with Veshadhari (those who express the emotion through costumes and make-up, as in the true Yakshagana). The Bhagavatha chooses the play to suit the particular limitations of this form. Acrobatics, fights, and strong movements are avoided. Argument, philosophy, literary exposition, and emotional interpretation are, however, ideally suited. The artists subtly interpret the roles and the meaning of the songs. The performer is something like a classical Kathak dancer who sits on the floor singing a *thumri* and interprets it through hand gestures and facial expressions. The Tala Maddale artists emphasize the emotional import. At times they lengthen the argument and go on with fine interpretations of the song, thereby shifting the emphasis from theatrical enjoyment to the more intellectual pleasures of an indoor seminar.

DODDATA

In such northern parts of Karnatak as Belgaum, Hubli, Dharwar, the Doddata (big play), another variant of Yakshagana, is popular. It is also called Bayalata (*bayal* = open air, *ata* = play) and is performed on a raised platform. Its themes are social satire, historical romance, and mythology.

The headdress of the hero is a six-inch-high cap with a spearlike crest. The songs are sung by the character himself since he does not have to dance vigorously. The background singer usually sings the refrain. The temperament is not *tandava* (heroic). In social plays women take part, but not in mythological ones.

Each play has a pivotal character who solves the problem. The hero and heroine are caught up in the grip of circumstance or chained by their own word or faith. In *Raja Harishchandra*, the truthful king suffers because he will not break his word of honor until the sage Vishwamitra appears to set him free of his bondage. In *Draupadi Cheer Haran* ("Stripping of Draupadi"), the heroine is on the verge of being stripped naked in the court of the Kauravas when Krishna comes to help her. In *Prahlada Charitra* ("The Story of the Boy-Saint Prahlada"), the boy is tortured by his father, Hiranyakashipu, for being a worshiper of the god. Just as he is being tied to a red-hot iron pillar, the lion-headed Narasimha appears and tears the power-drunk Hiranyakashipu with his claws. The savior enters from far off through the audience and jumps to the center of the stage.

The make-up of the main characters, Bhima, Ravana, Duryodhana, and Hiranyakashipu, is done in their homes or in the village *chavadi*, and they are brought to the arena in full splendor. The actor is led in a procession with music, drums, and oil torches. On the way the procession halts at different places where he dances wildly and shouts war cries. He is brought to the stage in a ceremonial din and is seated on a chair. He springs into action at the explosion of a firecracker.

Unlike Yakshagana, Doddata is full of boisterous humor. The dances are more rugged, the costumes gaudier, and the singing less varied than in Yakshagana. Doddata lacks weight and intensity. Its mythological tales lack the religious fervor of the Yakshagana. It is the social plays, the contemporary themes, the day-to-day life of the people that make this form effective.

Shivaram Karanth, playwright and noted authority on Yakshagana, has contributed much to preserve the authentic music and text of the original plays. However, in his experiments he abridges the long-winded songs and prose dialogue. In his production of *Bhishma Vijaya* ("Bhishma's Victory")—by shortening the ancient text, cutting down the songs, and concentrating on dance and mime—he has reduced the twelve-hour play to a two-and-a-half-hour dance-opera. In doing this, he has shifted its emphasis. A Yakshagana on a proscenium stage is robbed of its vigor. It is a different experience to see it in a coastal village. The music of the Bhagavatha has a quality of space. In a closed theater its shrivels. The *chande*, whose piercing clatter annoys the city audiences, is a necessity in the rural background. The pounding of the *chande*, its maddened vigor, its exultant abandon, urges the players to ferocious heights of dancing and acting.

Chapter Ten

CHHAU

THE TINY state of Seraikella, now a part of Bihar, has a ruggedly beautiful landscape. Circled by the Saranda and Bangriposi hills and fed by the Kharkai River, it never came under Moghul or Maratha domination. This gave it a sense of pride and aloofness. In 1820, when the rest of the Indian states, torn by strife, were being annexed by the British one by one, Seraikella signed a security treaty with the British. Untouched by foreign influence, it preserved its folk arts, native dances, and tribal mimes. Chhau, a unique form of masked dance-drama, is the specialty of this region.

The Seraikella rulers have always been actively associated with Chhau as patrons as well as performers. The finest exponent of the tradition today is Rajkumar Suddhendra, a thirty-four-year-old slim, sober man of humble temperament. His father, the eighty-year-old Maharaja Aditya Pratap Singh Deo, whose mind is a web of metaphysics, is the ultimate authority on Chhau. He approves the interpretations of the characters and gives final touches to the masks.

In Chhau the dancer impersonates a character—god, animal, bird, human being, rainbow, night, flower—and acts out a small theme. These dance-drama snippets are performed annually in April at the Chaitra Parva festival at Seraikella. The festival has elaborate rituals in honor of Kali (the Red and Black Kalis are impersonated by the head priest of the main Shiva temple) and celebrates the glory of Lord Shiva in his Ardhanarishwara* form, Shiva and Parvati in one. The entire village—royal household, priests, musicians, chanters, shopkeepers, farmers—participates in the ritual. The Chhau dances are performed in an aura of religious worship. But Chhau themes and methods of presentation have little to do with religion.

THE FESTIVAL

After consulting the horoscope of the maharaja and the movements of the stars, the astrologers fix the date for the festival, which lasts thirteen days. The first nine days are purely for ceremonies. On the last four days, along with rituals, the Chhau is performed in the courtyard of the royal palace in front of the Raghunath Temple dedicated to Rama, who was a devotee of Shiva.

The focal point of the rituals is Shiva's temple, standing in

---

* This composite form of Shiva revealing the male and the female in one—the two elements, the two opposite forces—has psychobiological truth. The Ardhanarishwara in the Elephanta Caves (on an island five miles off Bombay), twelve hundred years old, is a marvelous piece of sculpture in which Shiva and Parvati melt into each other, each retaining distinct characteristics and giving the image an aesthetic glory. The Ardhanarishwara dance is an important item of Chhau repertoire.

the heart of the town amidst the small shops of silversmiths, bangle-sellers, and toymakers, about 150 yards from the palace gate. On the first day, the Pujari (priest) hoists the *jarjara* (a red banner tied with mango leaves) and carries it ceremoniously from this temple to the Majna Ghat (royal bathing place) on the bank of the Kharkai River. Thirteen Bhaktas (devotees) chosen from different communities accompany him. Pipes, drums, and chanters follow. Worship is held in a temple on the river, after which the *jarjara* is brought back to Shiva's temple, taken to the palace courtyard where it is kept for some time in the Raghunath Temple, and again brought back to Shiva's temple. This ritual is repeated every evening for nine days until the main part of the festival starts.

After a ritualistic worship at the bathing ghat, a pitcher is filled with river water. A devotee from the community of oilmen, after fasting for a day and a night, bathes and purifies himself. He is then dressed in gory red. His arms, hands, legs, and face are painted the same color. The water pitcher is placed on his head and tightly fixed with cords so that it will not fall. Its top is decorated with plantain leaves and flowers, crested with a shining little crown. He is Mangala Chandi (auspicious Kali). The flutes blow, the drums shudder. People rush to the goddess and fall at her feet for blessings. Mangala Chandi, along with the *jarjara* bearer and Bhaktas and drummers and flutists, walks in a stylized gait to the palace courtyard. The procession swells as Mangala Chandi approaches his destination. On the way, charged with religious fervor, Mangala Chandi goes into a trance and capers and reels. People shower flowers on him. On reaching the palace courtyard where the maharaja sits, he dances more feverishly. The Bhaktas roll on a bed of thorns that has been spread to give them an occasion to express their devotion. This religious ecstasy is called *mal-garagari*. The Bhaktas are unhurt, partly by a miracle of faith and partly by training. After this Mangala Chandi proceeds to the main temple of Shiva accompanied by the *jarjara* bearer. The pitcher is taken off his head and placed near Shiva's linga. Then the performer and the Bhaktas break their fast with a sip of *charnamit* (the holy drink of the temple) and are fed. The *jarjara* is taken to the palace temple where it is kept to bless the Chhau dance at night. After the performance the *jarjara* is taken back to the temple of Shiva.

The following day the Brindabani ritual is performed. A man impersonating Hanuman repeats the devotion. No fasting or other elaborations are required. After the ceremony of placing the *jarjara* in the palace courtyard, the Chhau performance takes place. On the third day the Garia Bhar is observed. A performer carries two metal jars filled with water and walks in rhythmic steps from the river to the palace. Two females dressed in black and white saris flank him. A boy representing the child Krishna teases him on the way, dodges him, waylays him. On reaching the palace, all of them are received by the maharaja and given prominent seats to witness the Chhau.

On the fourth day the Kalika Ghat—the most ghoulish of ceremonies—takes place. A man in black, his face, hands, and legs painted pitch dark, represents the goddess Kali. After the usual ceremonies, amidst noisy music, he starts from the river and, dancing and tumbling, goes to the temple of Shiva. After this ceremony it is forbidden to perform the colorful Chhau, but if the royal family insists on a performance, it has to pay a small fine to the temple. The fine is gladly paid every year, and the performance is held. This custom insures the superior authority of the temple and the law-abiding tradition of the royal household.

On the fifth day Pat Sankranti is performed at the river.

Chhau masks

The chief devotee of the Shiva temple, wrapped in a red cloth, lies on a bed of curved iron nails, representing serpents. He represents a dead man bitten by a snake. The maharaja, arriving in a procession, touches the "corpse," and the royal touch revives the dead man. This ceremony is derived from a legend. Once a man died of a snake bite. The Maharaja of Seraikella saw Lord Shiva in a dream and was told by him to touch the man. He obeyed Shiva's order, and the man revived. To perpetuate the myth of the divine power of the ruler, the ceremony is conducted annually as a part of the festival. On this day there is no Chhau performance.

THE MASK

Chhau means "mask," an essential element in the dance-drama from which it derives its name. Etymologically, the Sanskrit word chhaya, "shadow" or "image," seems to be the root. Some claim that the word owes its origin to the chhauni (war camp) where the soldiers practiced the Parikhanda exercises that form part of the basic action poses of Chhau. A legend says that during the reign of Akbar the Great in the sixteenth century, the imperial army camping in the eastern regions of Bihar and Orissa got bored, and the high officials sought some form of entertainment. Some of them had studied music and dance. They evolved a dance form in which, by wearing masks and keeping mute, they could completely hide their faces and voices and thus keep their identities secret, for they did not want the lower ranks to recognize them. Their masked dances, crossbred with the local tribal mimes, resulted in the Chhau. This explanation seems farfetched since the dance is deeply wedded to the local traditions and war exercises of the soldiers of the region. It is still true, however, that the Chhau dancer wears a mask and keeps mute. No word is spoken, no song is sung. Only instrumental music accompanies the dance-drama.

The masks, with their flat pastel surfaces, avoid exaggeration, and for a novice it is difficult to distinguish one character from another. The symbolic curl of a lip or a little drunkenness in the eye or an almost imperceptible scowl sums up the individual. The mask has an abstract quality, a bland simplicity that may look dull. The body movements express the character's pain, inner turmoil, joy, anger.

In the dance-dramas of Kathakali, Therukoothu, and Bhagavatha Mela, the face is made up with intricate colors to focus the attention of the observer. The Chhau mask is static. It liberates the dancer-actor from the tyranny of speech and creates a hallucinatory relationship with reality. It projects life in the form of rhythms, harmonies, movements. Its austerity resembles the masks of *Ramayana* characters in Burma, which are also painted in flat colors. Even the lips are not painted red, and the eyebrows are not pronounced. Rama is pea-green, Lakshmana burnished gold. The *Ramayana* masks are kept in glass cases in family niches where they are worshiped. The Chhau mask has the same simplicity minus the religious flavor.

Chhau mask of the Swan

The Ardhanarishwara form of Shiva in Chhau is not represented in the traditional style by dividing the face into male and female sections. The face is expressed as one because in the Chhau conception Shiva and Parvati are one. Shiva's eyes, the three-pronged mark on the forehead, and the "third" eye express male energy and imagination. Below the nose, the lips have a small pout that expresses overpowering affection.

Animals, birds, planets, trees, seasons are characters. The Swan's face has a sharp nose and a crest, but no beak. The mask avoids realistic identification. The idea of a swan is given by its pursed lips, long tapering nose, and round red eyes

Radha and Krishna in a Chhau dance-drama

with yellow irises. The drooping eyes of Ratri (Night) suggest sleep. In *Banaviddha* ("The Arrow-struck Deer") the Deer's eyebrows are knit in anguish.

Krishna has many forms. In Chhau, Krishna, representing a brilliant child, has bright eyes, pouting lips, and a sensuous smile. The crown has peacock feathers and a tuft. The face is sky blue. The eyebrows, eyes, and lips bring out the essence of the character.

The Chhau mask is made of a dark clay found on the bank of the Kharkai River. This clay is pounded, strained, dissolved in water, and made into a thick paste. The clay model of the character is fixed on a small wooden plank and cooled for two or three days to harden it. A muslin gauze is pasted on it, and over the gauze two or three layers of paper; then again muslin, again paper, and over it a thick coating of the clay. The nose and eyes are fashioned by a sharp steel instrument (*karni*). After the mold is dry, the clay is scooped out from the hollow of the mask by the *karni* and the mask is scrubbed, polished, and painted. The famous maskmaker Parsanna Kumar Mahapatra, now sixty-five, lives in Seraikella under royal patronage. An expert craftsman, Mahapatra comes from a family that has been fashioning masks and figures for temples for four generations.

THEMES

Three different types of themes are used. *Hare-Vishnu*, *Madana-Gopala*, *Krishna-Balarama* have a religious background and are performed by young boys with simple dance steps, offering beginners a chance to be trained in the system. *Arati* ("Offering of Light"), *Dheebar* ("Fishermen"), *Astradanda* ("Sword Play"), and *Sabara* ("Hunter") give a glimpse of the social life. The choreography is based on the narrative description of the characters. The third, more developed and sophisticated, type has symbolism and philosophical interpretations. It is characterized by difficult movements, inner tension, and more vivid body expression. *Nabik* ("Boatman"), *Mayura* ("Peacock"), *Banaviddha* ("The Arrow-struck Deer"), and *Chandrabhaga* are in this category.

Nabik describes a man and a woman in a storm-tossed boat. The woman clings to the man for security. This gives the man strength to fight the storm. Sudden misery brings them together, and they emerge triumphant. The symbols of boat, river, and storm, which have been exploited by mystic poets, folk singers, and traditional dancers all over the world, are given a new vitality by the Chhau dancers. Rocking and swaying on the level stage, they give the impression of a wobbling boat. Their whirlwind movements, spiral steps, and hurried leaps create the storm. The abstract masks invest the scene with blinding power.

The Boatman and his Wife caught in a storm

Mayura is the idealized peacock. Its golden breast shows majesty and pride. The actor's blouse is made of golden net. His richly textured silk dhoti is blue. His hands and feet are dyed red. The dancer does not wear a tail, as do most traditional dancers portraying the peacock, but uses the blue-spotted feathery tail as a girdle. Sudden turns, startled gazes, knee-high strides, and nimble steps depict the bird. The luxurious hip movements used by primitive people to express joy are employed in this dance to reveal an inner surge of delight. The peacock is triumphant, proud, sensuous, vain. This interpretation was conceived by the late Kumar Bijoy Pratap Singh Deo, brother of the present maharaja. Now Rajkumar Suddhendra, in the role of Mayura, has added poignancy and sensuousness to the earlier conception.

Chandrabhaga, daughter of a sage, is bathing in the ocean. She is dedicated to the Moon Goddess. The Sun God, attracted by her beauty, pursues her. She spurns his overtures and finally jumps into the ocean and drowns She is the chaste woman who would rather commit suicide than submit to an unwanted male. The dance symbolizes the pursuing male and the rejecting woman. Chandrabhaga wears a half-moon disk with shafts of light at the back of her head. A small lotus-leaf crown adorns her forehead. The Sun God has a conical headgear and a large golden wheel fixed at his back.

The Chhau program is a variegated string of small dance-dramas, each lasting seven to ten minutes. The dance demands concentration and the focusing of the whole body, and it is exhausting if prolonged. Only men perform in Chhau. Even when the body expression is feminine, as in the case of the Boatwoman, Parvati, or Chandrabhaga, there is tension below the surface lyricism. Muscular spasms, streaming motions, and abrupt posturing require male energy.

The principal performing troupe is headed by Rajkumar Suddhendra and is patronized by his father the maharaja. The royal dancers of Khmer in Cambodia and the imperial Gagaku dancers of Japan follow a strict tradition of preserving the art in families, but Chhau does not. The Seraikella royal troupe lists artists from all classes and social strata and guards the tradition through the collective effort of the community.

The mask of the Peacock (Mayura) worn by Rajkumar Suddhendra

Recently the Rajkumar composed a short dance-drama, *Megha-doot* ("Cloud-Messenger"), based on a long poem by Kalidasa. In it, Mountain, Cloud, Rainbow, Yaksha, Yakshi —each has been given a mask with a stylized costume. The Cloud carries a flashing sword (symbolizing lightning) and a shield (thunder). In the parting scene between the two lovers, Yaksha and Yakshi, the dominant rasa (sentiment) is created by the magic of pure body expressions.

The Peacock dances with pride and majesty

The Rajkumar said: "When I put on the mask I become impersonal. It is easier to slip into the body of another character. The face is not required to express. It passes its function to the body. Expression does not flow from my face to my body, but is transmitted from my body to my face."

UPALAYAS

Some of the Chhau dance steps are taken from the war dance Parikhanda (*pari* = shield, *khanda* = sword). This was a popular exercise in war camps to keep the soldiers fit and to train them in sword and shield play, and in earlier times some of the Chhau dancers were expert soldiers in Parikhanda.

The basic stance is as follows: the right and left foot are placed on the floor at right angles to each other, with the heel of the left foot facing the middle of the right foot; the knees are bent outward; the left arm is extended with the hand lowered; the right arm bends at the elbow at a right angle forward,

the hand holding a sword toward the sky. The whole body is at right angles, the arms, the legs, the knees, the feet. From the waist upward the dancer has a fighter's pose, with chest thrown out and chin tilted as if he were alertly watching the opponent. The walk is that of a prowling animal. With the right arm extending forward, the left knee lunges forward in a springy walk. The same action is repeated in walking backward and sideward.

Parikhanda exercises are vigorous, agile, acrobatic. They call for the split-second timing, sharp turns, and baffling postures employed by the warrior of olden times to dodge his opponent. The exercise begins with a number of *chalis,* styles of walk. These are in single, double, and quadruple tempi and are forward, backward, and sideward, named after the style of the steps: *archi-chali* is a crosswise step, and *teenparhi-chali* is three steps in a single time sequence. Some *chalis* are inspired by the gaits of animals and birds. Examples are: *bagh-chali,* the walk of a tiger; *bhalu-chali,* the walk of a bear; *gau-mutra-chali,* the walk of a cow while urinating; *bug-chali,* the walk of a crane; *ghora-tabuka,* a horse trot; *chheli-dian,* a goat jumping; *harini-dian,* a deer jumping; *bagh-pani-khia,* a tiger drinking water. These *chalis* and *dians,* combined with other body movements, express various actions called *upalayas.* *Upalayas* form the basic vocabulary. They are copied from the activities of human beings, birds, and animals. The feet and the legs are the most expressive parts of the body in this dance style.

The feet of a Chhau dancer have a gesture language. His toes are agile, functional, expressive. Animals use their feet as dextrously as their hands, and the Chhau dancer understands this. His feet not only supply a drum rhythm to other parts of the body which become the main vehicle of expression, but stand as self-conscious instruments of feelings and actions.

The following *upalayas* are taken from women working, washing, dressing: *gooti-koorha* (picking pebbles), *kharkibar* (sweeping the floor), *gobar-goola* (mixing and slapping cow dung), *kula-pachra* (husking rice), *bota-cheera* (splitting a bamboo), *pitho-bata* (grinding a stone), *jhoonti-dian* (making designs on the floor), *gaddhi-jiba* (going to bathe), *pahur-maja* (cleaning anklets), *khadu-maja* (cleaning bracelets), *sindur-tika* (putting the sacred vermilion mark on the forehead).

The feet perform these actions with rare grace and nimbleness. They sweep the floor, pick up pebbles, and make designs. To express the *sindur-tika,* the dancer swings the right foot to the forehead, the toe touching it effortlessly. By this acrobatic movement the whole body comes into action and expresses the theme with grace and surprise, as if a coiled cane were released.

About one hundred such *upayalas* and *chalis* (walks) were in the Chhau gesture repertoire, but now hardly fifty are known and practiced.

Parikhanda exercises are held traditionally at sunrise on the bank of the Kharkai River at a place dedicated to Lord Shiva. Seven lingas sanctify the place. The performers place their swords and shields before the linga and prostrate themselves, paying homage to Lord Shiva and seeking his blessings. Then they pick up the swords and shields, kiss them reverently, and jump into the arena. The guru, like a drill master, conducts the Parikhanda exercises. The performers' torsos are bare. They drape their white dhotis tightly around their hips and gather the folds and tuck these up in front inside their girdles so that their legs can be freely parted for swift and smooth action. The guru chants the mnemonic syllables and guides their movements. The performers mumble the same syllables to concentrate on the steps.

All dances are in three tempi: *vilambit* (slow), *madhya* (medium), and *drut* (fast), with a few exceptions such as *Phool-basant* ("Flowers of Spring"), which has only slow and fast rhythms.

Song compositions of famous Oriya poets—Upendra Bhanja, Kabi Surya, Uddita Narayana—have been used by the Chhau performers. By discarding the words of the song, they get to the essence. The melody has an evocative quality. The songs of a boatman, rain, a storm, a peacock, separation and parting are a part of the literary and musical background of the people. When the flute plays the melody, the spectators are unconsciously aware of the original words. Vague echoes ring in their minds, pictures pulsate, images throb. The Chhau dancers fully exploit this evocative power.

A change in tempo is always preceded by a *katan*, a triple blaze of rhythmic beat, which serves as a transition. The duration of a performance depends upon the will of the dancer. If he wants to conclude it earlier or chooses to change the tempo or move from one rhythm pattern to another or from one sequence to a different one, he gives a meaningful nod to the instrumentalists, who catch the hint.

The guru sits near the instrumentalists and speaks out drum *bols* (rhythmic syllables), controlling the tempo. Sometimes he gets up to adjust the mask of a character, tighten the arrow-filled quiver at his back, or fix the large gilded wheel of the Sun God. The instrumentalists sit behind the performers. The maharaja, the members of his family, and chosen guests sit in the front. The commoners sit to the right and left of the stage. Behind the instrumentalists sit the poor. The principal instruments are a large kettledrum (*dhamsa*), a pipe terminating in a bulge (*mahuri*), and cymbals.

The Chhau performers have two *akharas*: the Bazar Shahi Akhara, patronized by the royal family, and the Brahmin Akhara, controlled by the leading Brahmin families. Each has four branches. They compete at the annual Chaitra Parva festival.

Chhau is highly stylized. It does not permit rustic crudity.

The interpretation of most themes is metaphysical. The rhythms occasionally have difficult patterns; the music abounds in classical *ragas*. Most commonly used melodies are the *des* and *malkauns* because the dance is vigorous. The invocation is generally done in *des ragini*. Since the art developed under the patronage of the royal court, it has a gilded, classical flavor.

In spite of all these ingredients, Chhau has a strong undercurrent of folk elements. At the annual festival, troupes representing different neighborhoods take part, each performing eight to ten items. It has elaborate ritualistic celebrations which plunge the entire town into a mass dance-drama activity. The mask itself is simple, with one flat color that gives it a naïve quality of frankness, simplicity, boldness. Some of the themes danced by young boys are taken directly from the existing folk forms. The use of the plain mask, the dance's short duration and lack of elaboration place it between the two extremes, the classical and the folk.

The neighboring state of Mayurbhanj, now a part of Orissa, preserves a Chhau form in which actors do not wear masks. Their facial expression is static, deliberately stiff and immobile, like a mask. It is much more vigorous and rustic than the Seraikella style. A dozen troupes of male dancers are active in the Mayurbhanj area. Each troupe has about thirty members and is nonprofessional. The members are betel-sellers, rickshaw-pullers, peddlers, woodcutters. During the rule of the former Maharaja of Mayurbhanj, the two Chhau styles were rivals. The gurus taught the dance with keen discipline. Today the troupes are subsidized by the Mayurbhanj Chhau Nrutya Pratisthan of the Baripada District, which abounds in tribal hunts and mimes. The Pratisthan pays five to six rupees per head per month to each member of the recognized troupes so that they may keep the tradition alive.

The Mayurbhanj style is jerky, vigorous, and has acrobatic freedom. The dancer wriggles his hips and knees, jumps, trots, and walks with high strides. Suddenly he slows to nimble steps and stalks as if about to murder a man in the dark. The warrior wears crossbands on his chest, a tightly draped dhoti, a sash running across the shoulder down the waist and tied at the back, and holds a stick.

The program often includes the following. *Dhajatal* is a wild, springy, erratic tribal dance that has been given a Chhau pattern by adding to it knee movements and light steps. *Sabara* depicts a hunter in a forest. Finding the footprints of a tiger, the hunter tracks it down, kills it with a spear, and carries the dead animal home. He walks under the weight of the tiger, feels tired and thirsty, puts down the tiger, drinks from a

stream, and dances with joy. In *Jambeb* the dancer-actor impersonates a bear by dressing like a prehistoric hairy man with
black face and claws. At first he crouches with his hands
covering his face, his wild, fiery eyes peering from behind his
hands. Suddenly he springs into action. His movements create
the thick forest where he roams in search of prey. He brings
out the ferocity of the bear, a remarkable feat of acting.

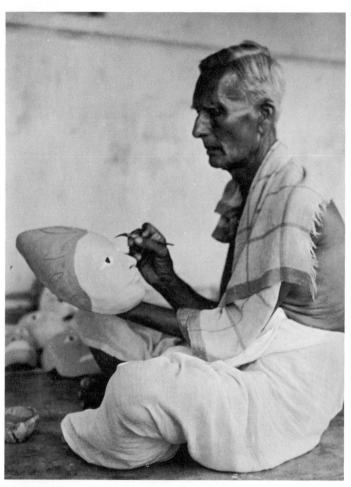

The mask maker Parsanna Kumar Mahapatra

Chapter Eleven

GLIMPSES OF OTHER FORMS

A NUMBER of folk theatrical forms are scattered all over India, ranging from the highly evolved traditional dance-dramas to the tribal hunt mimes. Most are not so well developed as those described in previous chapters, but they are nevertheless interesting. The dance-dramas of Bhagavatha Mela and Kuchipudi of South India, the Ankia Nat (sixteenth-century one-act play) of Assam, the farcical Naqal of Punjab, the Bhand Jashna of Kashmir, the Bheel Gauri of Rajasthan, the Veedhi-natakam of Andhra, and the Pala singers of Orissa form a part of the general study of the folk theater. Some of the tribal mimes and ritualistic dances have been studied by anthropologists, but to a student of theater they are revealing in costume, gesture, mime, rhythms, postures, and make-up.

The relationship of the classical and the folk is deeply knit in South India. A good folk actor knows the *Shastras*, the *Puranas*, the epics, and the scriptures on classical dance and music. In the north—the Punjab, Kashmir, Rajasthan—he is steeped in the folklore and is mostly ignorant of the classical tradition. The south has a religious and mythological background; the north has a secular temperament.

The Punjab has no solid tradition of religious pageant drama as does Uttar Pradesh with its Ramlila and Krishnalila cycle plays. The genius of the Punjabi people finds expression in love stories, lusty dancing, and humor. Naqal (farce) is a centuries-old tradition in the villages, enacted by Bhands, the village buffoons. Two or three people constitute a troupe. The leader holds a leather folder in his hand to slap his partner with at a climactic moment. They are dressed in rustic clothes—a turban, a loose-sleeved shirt, and a *tehmad* (saronglike short dhoti). Sometimes one of them carries a hookah. In a small arena they perform a series of Naqals, each lasting hardly ten minutes, full of snappy questions and answers.

They go round and round talking, repeating, snapping at each other, and leading the audience from suspense to the final explosion of an absurdly hilarious point. Typical themes are the newly-wed bride and the father-in-law; the king and his courtier; the thief and the police inspector; the schoolteacher and his pupil; the weaver and his mother-in-law; the stupid soldier and his general; the old miser and his young wife.

One of the popular Naqals is about a father and his daughter. The daughter pouts, kicks, and simpers, begging her father to find her a bridegroom. The father has arranged everything, and the wedding party is arriving:

Daughter: I am happy ... very happy, father, I wish that my wedding party would arrive ...
Father: In bullock carts?

Daughter: Only weavers travel in bullock carts!

Father: Then on horses?

Daughter: Only clowns ride horses.

Father: On camels?

Daughter: Who would ride the humped beast?

Father: Then on elephants?

Daughter: You want my bridegroom to fall and break his back?

Father: What mode of travel do you want?

Daughter: I want, father . . . I want, father . . . they should soon arrive.

Father: In motor cars?

Daughter: Motor cars get punctures and go flat.

Father: Then on what?

Daughter: I want, father, I want the wedding party to arri—

Father: In an airplane?

Daughter: An air crash—and I shall be a widow!

Father (puzzled): What conveyance shall I arrange for your wedding party, dear daughter?

Daughter: Rats—on which the god Ganesha rides!

At her foolish answer the father slaps her with the leather folder, and she runs wildly around the arena.

In *Mochi de Ghar Chori* ("Theft in a Cobbler's House"), the police inspector comes to conduct an investigation. The frightened cobbler hides behind his wife's skirt:

Inspector: How did you know that a thief had burgled?

Wife: Pearly one, I heard the haystack barking and saw it running toward the dog.

Inspector: What did you do then?

Wife: Great sire, I jumped out of my bed. Immediately I rolled my skirt and put on the bed around my waist.

Inspector: Then what happened?

Wife: May God bless you with a dozen children! Then I saw the courtyard rushing past the thief.

Cobbler (peeping from behind): Sir, she is trembling with fear. If you permit m-m-m . . . if you per—

Inspector: Bark!

Cobbler: May the plume of your turban . . .

Inspector: Be brief! Tell me what have you lost?

Cobbler: Sir, I have lost nine yards of my cow, and the black-hoofed turban is . . .

The leader slaps the cobbler with his folder for his stupid replies. The audience shrieks with laughter.

The buffoon exploits all the tricks: exaggeration, repetition,

absurdity, malapropism, fantastic lies. His gags, comic remarks, lewd references, and euphemistic comments make the
arena bubble with laughter. Inventive and witty, he de-
molishes his opponent with a phrase. If the troupe is performing before a prince or a landlord, the buffoon begs pardon
in advance from his patrons before he lashes them with his
wit. In ancient times kings and landlords kept such buffoons
around them. The popular character of Vidushaka in Sanskrit
plays is the first cousin of the village Bhand. The Moghul
emperor Akbar the Great had the wisest wit, Raja Birbal, as
one of the "nine jewels" in his court. Maharaja Ranjit Singh,
the mighty Sikh ruler of the nineteenth century, was fond of
jokes at his own expense if they were by a really brilliant
buffoon and would reward him with gold coins.

The Buffoon in the Punjabi Naqal

For the most part, Mirasis—Muslim artist clowns—were
the preservers of this tradition. There is a saying that a Mirasi
would rather lose his wife than a good joke. The vocation was
hereditary. The son learned the art by watching his father

perform and joined him at an early age, thus absorbing all the stock characters and situations that the father exploited. After the Partition these Muslim artists moved to Pakistan, leaving the rural theatrical scene of the Punjab devoid of humor and color.

The Kashmir Valley is an eighty-by-twenty-mile oval of lakes, paddy fields, saffron plots, and floating gardens. Its songs and dances have the quiet of a lake. The delicate Hafiza and Rouf dances of the women and the Bacha Nagma of the young boys are characterized by slow turns and gentle swaying. The modern Kashmiri-language theater was born after 1947, though they have a folk theater, Bhand Jashna (Festival of Bhands) that is three or four hundred years old. Muslim rulers, because of their religious tenets, discouraged sculpture and the dramatic arts, but music flourished in their courts. Zain-ul-Abdin (fifteenth century) invited dancers and singers from distant lands to annual festivals. Later Ali Shah and Hassan Shah patronized the arts. Bhand Jashna evolved from the folk traditions and royal patronage. The plays are called *pather* (perhaps from *patra* which means a scroll), and Bhand is the vernacular form of the classical Bhandika, meaning a clown. Bhand Pather deals with social realities and makes use of dance, music, clowning, and satire. It is performed in the village square. A musical prelude is sung by four or five performers after which lively characters, humorous anecdotes, and caricatures are presented interspersed with singing and dancing. Pather mirrors social evils: the cunning moneylender, the dowry system, the corrupt police, the haughty officials. It includes farces about a sweeper, a peasant, a king, a barber, a monk. Some plays are about legendary heroes and gallant lovers. But it is the incisive satire that characterizes Bhand Jashna, giving relief to people who have led hard lives under the monarchs and maharajas.

The Bheels of Rajasthan perform a ceremonial dance, Gouri, in the month of Bhadrapad in honor of their deity Budia. It expresses the tribal impulses, the urge to dance, sing, mime, and enjoy the performance for its own sake. The Gouri players feel insulted if anyone offers to pay them.

The Gouri has a special function as a meeting of the people of two villages. When a woman from one village marries a man from another and goes there to live with him, a group of Gouri players from her own area will come to her new home at the time of the festival to perform. This may be done soon after the wedding or many years later, or they may make annual visits as a community greeting. The players fix the *trishul* (trident) in the ground, reminiscent of the god Indra's flagstaff in the ancient plays, beat the drum and pound a bronze plate so that the whole village, and especially the woman, knows that the Gouri party has come. The people sit clustered in the arena. The woman greets the players with a coconut, a silver coin, and an offering to the deity.

It is a full-day performance, starting at sunrise and ending at sunset. The dancers wear gourd masks and carry swords and shields. Primitive masks, vigorous singing, and spirited action are specialties of this form. Thousands of people witness the shows. The ritual is vitally connected with their social customs, dance forms, and religious motifs.

VEEDHI-NATAKAM

Andhra is rich in traditional dance-dramas. The main form of the folk traditional theater is Veedhi-natakam (*veedhi* means street, *natakam* a play), also called Veedhi-bhagavatam. Yenadi-bhagavatam is danced, sung, and acted by the aboriginal Yenadi tribe. They have dark skin, flat noses, kinky hair, and strong Negroid elements. Their dance has wild rhythms. Golla-bhagavatam is performed by shepherds and milkmen. Legends, epic tales, and myths are the themes of their dance-dramas. In Dasari-bhagavatam the untouchable class celebrates the worship of its deities and gods. In the performance they introduce local events, jokes, caste problems, and contemporary color. Jakkula-bhagavatam, performed by a sect of devotees, popularizes celestial and folk legends.

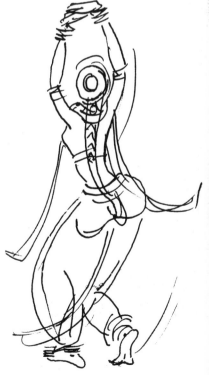

These four forms of Veedhi-natakam have a loose structure. The costume colors are loud. Make-up is yellow, lemon or ocher mixed with coconut oil to give the face a dark sheen. Eyes and eyelashes are lampblacked. Jute fibers dyed black are used for beards and mustaches. Women wear gilded pith ornaments, beads, and necklaces, and saris of deep red, yellow, or green. The plays are performed in the street with crude acting and language understandable to the common man. Some of the actors cannot read and write. Of the four forms, only in Jakkula-bhagavatam do women take part.

In these folk plays, the Sutradhara sings, introduces the characters, comments in prose, and is a link between the drama and the audience. He carries a *kutilaka*, a curved S-shaped bamboo stick.* He is a director-narrator-buffoon in one. He jokes with the spectators as well as with the characters. Hold-

---

* The stick is heated and kept tied by a string for some days until it becomes S-shaped. The Vidushaka of Sanskrit plays carries this curved stick.

ing *talam* (tiny metal cymbals) in his hands, he sings and keeps time and narrates the events. While singing he tucks the *kutilaka* under his arm or lets it hang down his shoulder. At the opening of the play he sings a song honoring the deity, eulogizes the patron, and thanks him for arranging the show.

Yaksha (Jakkula) and Nagavasi are two communities in Andhra that have been dedicated to dance and music since ancient times. The Yakshas developed the tradition of Yakshagana, which differs from that of Kanara. In Kanara the Bhagavatha is the principal singer. The actors do not sing most of the time because they are required to dance a lot. In Andhra the dancer-actor leads the song, assisted by the singing chorus, called Sahakaragan (helper-singer). The hero wears a conical crown with large brackets on both sides extending outward, and a billowy skirt, and carries a handkerchief and a sword. When he wants to express the *bhava*, he puts down the sword and handkerchief. This form lacks the gilded vigor and musical refinement of the Kanara Yakshagana.

Pagati Bhagavathulu (daytime play) in its earlier stages portrayed mainly events in Krishna's life. With the passage of time the common people have become the subject of this form. Like the Pagal Vesham of Tamilnad, it is performed during the daytime. The main art lies in impersonation. The actor dresses as a retired judge, a Muslim fakir, a moneylender, a village headman, an oppressed wife, instilling the role with a light humor. Vedantam Chantayya, his son Malikarjuna, and his grandsons are the chief actors of this form.

There are also short thirty-minute tableaux, representing diverse social characters, that are repeated five or six times during the night. The spectators are a floating group. An incident from the epics comes to life offering color, good costume, strong make-up, exaggeration. The actors arrange themselves in a pictorial composition while the music is sung, commenting on the scene. During religious celebrations and full-moon festivals, these performances are particularly popular in southeast Andhra.

Bayal-nataka uses a three-tiered stage with rope ladders for the actors. It is an open-air performance. Its high-tiered platform stage gives it the feeling of a pageant play. The stories are from mythology, and the action is usually carried on in different areas simultaneously. The people know the story and can understand and enjoy the multiple action at different stage levels. In Varanasi Ramlila the multiple-set stage is arranged in different areas of the arena. In Bayal-nataka the stage levels are constructed vertically to create a manifold vision of action. The best actors of this form are in Gadwal village, sixty miles from Hyderabad.

An interesting form of enactment of the *Ramayana* story, Chirtal Ramayana, is popular in Alwal and other villages around Secunderabad. A group of people in splendid costume and make-up perform the epic story in two concentric circles. At the climax, the players join in a community dance.

BURRAKATHA

Burrakatha is a dramatic ballad sung by three people. *Burra* is a hollowed pumpkin instrument with four strings. The *burra* player uses two bronze rings set with metallic bells on his thumb to give the beat. He leads the song, gesticulating, emphasizing the words with his facial expression, jumping backward and forward. Suddenly he stops in a crouching posture and sings first in whispers and then in a high-pitched voice. His two companions playing on small drums sing and question in prose and poke fun and draw out the story.

The leader wears ankle bells and executes acrobatic dance phrases between the narrative parts. The themes are tales of chivalry and legendary heroes. The most famous is *Bobbili Yuddham* ("Battle of Bobbili"). In bygone days the French have occupied the coastal parts of Andhra. A Hindu king joins hands with the French and destroys the Bobbili fort. The heroine, Queen Mallama, wife of Raja Rangarao of Bobbili, burns herself to death to save her chastity. The Burrakatha singers, expert in evoking the past, have kept the traditional tales of patriotism alive in rural areas.

Kuchipudi dancer Vedantam Satyanarayana applying his make-up

KUCHIPUDI

Kuchipudi dance-dramas owe their origin to a small village, Kuchipudi (Kuchelapuram). The form was originated by Siddhendra Yogi, creator of the superb dance-drama *Bhama Kalapam* (the story of charming Satyabhama, wife of Lord Krishna, who is jealous of Rukmini's love). He is considered to be a disciple of the saint-poet Tirtha Narayan Yati, who composed *Krishna Leela Tarangini* ("The River of Krishna's Amorous Sports").

Siddhendra Yogi taught the art to Brahmin boys of Kuchipudi and showed a performance to the Nawab of Golconda (1675). The Nawab was so pleased that he granted Kuchipudi village to the Brahmin Bhagavathas for the preservation of the art. Even today every Brahmin of Kuchipudi village is expected to perform at least once in his life the role Satyabhama. This is a sort of offering to Lord Krishna for the preservation of the art in the village. Shri Chinta Krishnamurthi heads the most expressive troupe of Kuchipudi artists and plays the Su-

Vedantam Satyanarayana as the charming Satyabhama

tradhara. He enlivens the production by his inspired singing.
In his troupe young Vedantam Satyanarayana portrays Satyabhama with subtle shades of jealousy, anger, and love unsurpassed by any other artist. When Satyanarayana plays the role,
anyone except his wife can watch him because it is believed
that his impersonation of Satyabhama will be injured if his
wife sees him in the garb of a charming woman.

Kuchipudi starts with rituals. First a man dances, sprinkling
holy water. Incense is burnt to sanctify the stage. Afterward
Indradhwaja (Indra's flagstaff) is planted on the stage to
guard the performance against outside interference. Women
carry worship lamps and sing and dance, followed by an offering of flowers. The Sutradhara, the singer-narrator-Bhagavatha,
announces the play. The worship of Ganesha follows. The
Sutradhara sings the invocation to the goddess Balatripura-
sundari, Saraswati, Lakshmi, and a prayer song to Parashakti
(Parent Energy). In between he chants the drum syllables.

Two men hold up the traditional colored curtain. A long gold-embroidered braid is hung on the curtain as a challenge to anyone among the spectators who dares to act and dance. If anyone takes up this braid, the hero playing the female character Satyabhama will cut off "her" hair. The principal characters are introduced from behind the curtain after each one has done a brisk dance while the Sutradhara sings out the background, function, and role of the character.

The Bhagavatha and Satyabhama in the Kuchipudi dance-drama Bhama Kalapam

The performance is lyrical in temperament. All roles are played by men. Superb musical compositions give scope to expressive acting. All four elements of abhinaya are used—angika (body), vachika (song), aharya (costume), and sattvika (psychological resources of the actor)—as mentioned in the Natyasastra, the two-thousand-year-old book of Hindu dramaturgy. Because of its popularity, the form is called Kuchipudi Veedhinatakam.

BHAGAVATHA MELA

The traditional dance-drama Bhagavatha Mela is performed annually at the Narasimha Jayanti festival in Melattur village in Tamilnad. It uses the classical gesture language with a dense Karnatak musical fabric. The tradition that was earlier practiced in six villages around Tanjore—Melattur, Soolimanga-

lam, Uttukaddu, Nallur, Saliyamangalam, and Theperuma-
nallur—has shrunken and taken the form of a ritual at Melattur
in the service of the god Narasimha.

The tradition, which was richly followed during the rule of
the Nayak and Maratha kings of Tanjore, has declined. Today
the form is appreciated by connoisseurs and has been reclaimed
as a traditional dance-drama style. Bhagavatha Mela was given
a new life by the composer Venkatarama Sastri (1759–1847),
a contemporary of Tyagaraja, the great saint-singer of South
India. Sastri composed marvelous dance-dramas in the Telugu
language and enriched the repertoire. The most famous of his
immortal works is *Prahlada Charitram.*

At the annual festival, held in May-June, the deity is taken
out in an evening procession and ceremoniously installed in
the *gopuram* passage. The players perform all night on a platform before the presiding deity.

The opening benediction (*todiyamangalam*) is followed by
Konangi (the Clown), who capers and tumbles. Then the
chamberlain of the royal palace appears and announces the
hero. The Bhagavatha leads the chorus and reads out a description of each character, and the singers offer the introductory
song called *daru* (Bharata Muni called the introductory songs
pravesika dhruvas). These *darus* are excellent *raga* compositions in slow rhythm ideally suited for interpretative acting.

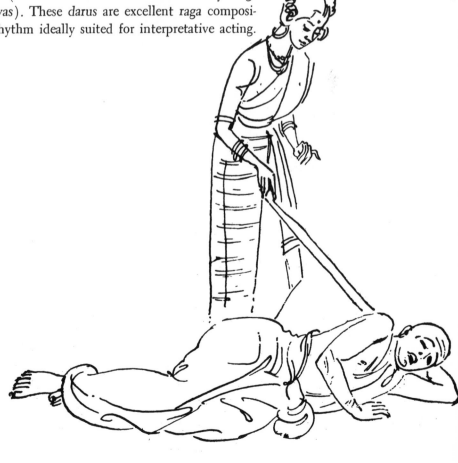

The *daru* gives the idea of the character, the mood, the background. Every character—a king, a queen, a hermit, a fool—enters dancing to the *daru*. Singers sing out the lines acted out by the character. The Bhagavatha reader connects the scenes by chanting prose pieces. The characters do a brief dance as the Bhagavatha sings the introduction. The play goes on all night, using a gesture language accompanied by strong dance and music.

All the players are devotees, employed in different places. They assemble at the festival from far and wide and offer their homage by performing in the temple. Women are not allowed to appear on the stage. The actors inherit the art and preserve the tradition. The mask of the god Narasimha in the *Prahlada Charitram* is preserved in the temple of Varadaraja Perumal and worshiped daily. The person acting the god Narasimha purifies himself by fasting all day. At the climax of the play, when Narasimha appears out of the pillar to tear apart Hiranyakashipu's belly, he thunders and often goes into a frenzy.

KURAVANJI

Kuravanji is a dance-drama of lyrical beauty prevalent in Tamilnad. Four to eight women perform it. It is about a lovesick lady pining for her lover who is always the king or the deity in whose honor the dance-drama is being enacted. A gypsy fortuneteller informs the lady how she will meet her lover. The Kuravanji takes its name from the Tamil word *kura*, meaning "gypsy." The other women are *sakhis*, friends of the heroine. The hero, though constantly mentioned, never appears. Though the theme and its treatment have a folk quality, the

dance and music are highly classical as in the Bharata Natyam form of this region.

ANKIA NAT

Assam has preserved Ankia Nats (one-act plays) written by the saint-poet Shankaradeva (1449–1568) and his disciple, Madhavdeva (1489–1596). They introduced music, dance, and acting as important features in their worship of Vaishnava gods, principally Krishna. The Sutradhara sings the invocation song through gesture and dance, introduces the story, and sings a song as each principal character enters, giving his background and function. He is the most important character in this dramatic form. He tells the audience "to watch and listen attentively." He wears a white skirt over tight-fitting *chooridar* pajamas, a lotus-pink shirt with flapping sleeves, a turban, and a girdle. His dress is more traditional in form and style than that of the other characters.

Ankia Nats are rich in literary content and song and have been most effective in propagating the lore of Krishna and stories of his childhood. Shankaradeva exploited the old form, Ojapali, in which the main character, Oja, sings the story and converses in prose with the chief Pali, while other members of the company sing and dance. This rudimentary combination of dance with musical narrative was the chief traditional form of dramatic art. Shankaradeva and his disciple created a rich one-act play form that was far ahead of their times. They used Braj, the pan-Indian language of Vaishnava saints, ideally suited for the expression of spiritual beauty. At the time when Ashta Chhap saint-poets were creating superb poetry in the Braj area in the north, Shankaradeva evolved a dramatic form in Assam and linked it with the literary tradition of the north. Famous plays by him and his disciples are: *Kaliya Daman* ("The Subjugation of the Serpent Kaliya"), *Patni Prasad* ("The Appeasement of the Housewives"), *Rasa Krida* ("The Ras Dance of Krishna"), *Rukmini Haran* ("Abduction of the Charming Rukmini"), *Sriram Vijaya* ("Rama's Victory"), *Parijata Haran* ("The Bringing of the Parijata Tree"), and *Sri Krishna Janma* ("Birth of Krishna").

Up until the beginning of this century, Assamese drama was kept alive only by the Ankia Nats. Today these are still performed, sung, and danced in monasteries and temples.

PALAS AND DASKATHIAS

The Pala actors and Daskathias of Orissa are powerful dramatic singers.

Five to six people form a Pala singing team. The leader, Mukhya Gayak (Principal Singer), wears a magenta turban, a

peacock crest, and earrings. He holds brass bells in his right hand, and in his left hand carries a *chanwar* (a bushy fly whisk made of the hair of a black deer). Three musicians hold large cymbals; another plays on the *hatha-kathi* (a wooden instrument held in the hand and producing a rhythmic clatter); one plays on the *mridangam* (horizontal drum). All the musicians wear colored petticoats, blouses, silver chest decorations, and a girdle. They look strangely female with masculine vigor. They are the female partners (Gopis) of Krishna, represented by the principal singer who sings the narrative and dances.

A Juang tribal woman in Orissa

The female partners sway their hips, move in a stylized manner, and reinforce the song of the leader with a musical groan of "*hain-hain-hain.*" They clang the cymbals as they reel about. The leader raises his hand, and they stop. Then he speaks in rhythmic prose, and the Gopis underline his words with "*oh-oh-oh.*"

The Pala actors perform to rural audiences on an arena stage at ground level. The Palas are musical dramas, stories from mythology and history. The principal singer-actor puts questions, narrates, and sings. Without changing his dress, he plays many characters. One moment he may be speaking the words of Krishna, but then the singing changes, the opposite character becomes Krishna, and the Pala leader becomes Draupadi or Arjuna. After a while he swings back to the role of Krishna. This multiple changing of characters is accomplished by fast-changing moods and clear-cut gestures. The leader is a scholar of Oriya literature; he is a good singer and is well versed in Sanskrit, music, and dance. He quotes copiously from Sanskrit poets and Oriya writers. An energetic performer, he grimaces and jumps about. When in good form, he sometimes springs five feet high.

The Daskathias, a team of two players, sing heroic ballads. They jump and gesticulate and spring backward and forward, powerfully charging the atmosphere. In their hands they hold a clattering instrument made of two flat pieces of wood. This gives rhythm and tempo to their spirited singing. They circulate the heroic ballads in villages and form a singer-narrator team of excellent actors.

PUPPETS

Puppet theater is perhaps the oldest form of theater.

The Putliwalas of Rajasthan operate marionettes which are light-moving dolls made of wood and bright-colored cloth. The themes are of kings, lovers, bandits, and princesses. Generally the puppeteer and his nephew or son operate the strings from behind while the puppeteer's wife sits on her haunches in front of the miniature stage, playing on the drum and commenting on the action. The character of Sutradhara (meaning "holder of strings") in Sanskrit plays seems to have been derived from the puppet theater in which the director holding the strings controls the interaction of characters and their emotions. The Putliwala chirps and whimpers and squeals in a funny animal-bird voice and creates battles and tragic moments, expressing pathos, separation, anger, and laughter.

Andhra offers quite a different type of puppetry. The puppets, fashioned of colored translucent leather, are called Tholu Bommalata (the dance of leather dolls). These are projected on a small screen like color transparencies. Animals, birds, gods, and demons dominate the screen. The puppeteer manipulates the puppets from behind the screen with two sticks. Strong lamps are arranged so that the size, position, and angle of the puppets change with the distance of the light. These have similarities with the Wayang Kulit of Indonesia. While the Indonesian puppets are large, the Andhra figures are small and quick-moving. Mythological tales and legends have been revived in a very live theatrical form by the Andhra puppeteers.

Muria tribal girls dancing at a wedding party. Photograph by Dr. Verrier Elwin

FOLK COLOR IN MODERN DRAMA

Lately there has been a stress on folk culture in India. Every year on Republic Day dancers from all parts of the country, ranging from the tribal Murias of Madhya Pradesh to the lyrical Lambadi women of Andhra, perform in the National Stadium and parade in the streets. Annual folk song contests are held. Handicraft exhibits are organized in big centers. But folk theater is still a neglected art.

In the West, writers and directors are borrowing from the traditional Asian theater a repertoire of stylization—the use of song, dance, mime, rituals, masks, and the narrator. The most obvious example is Bertolt Brecht, whose Epic Theater was directly influenced by the Peking Opera, the Kabuki, and folk forms. Indian directors, while recognizing Brecht's theatrical wizardry, have been reluctant to explore the raw material of their own traditional theater. Only recently some of them have come to recognize and employ folk techniques in their work.

In the absence of a powerful city theater (barring a few houses in Calcutta, Bombay, and Madras), the folk theater has kept the hungry audiences of 700,000 villages entertained for centuries and played an important part in the growth of modern theaters in different language areas. The nineteenth-century dramatist Bharatendu Harishchandra, who was responsible for the birth of Hindi drama, used folk conventions —*mangalacharana*, tableaux, comic interludes, duets, stylized speech—and combined these with Western theatrical forms of that time. The most powerful commercially run Parsi theatrical companies adapted the popular folk techniques for their extravaganzas. They were a major influence until 1930. Rabindranath Tagore, the brilliant playwright-composer-actor-director, mocked the commercial Bengali theater, burdened with heavy sets and realistic décor, and created a lyrical theater of the imagination. He was much influenced by Vaishnava poets, Keertans, Baul singers, and folk actors. Jatra flavor is clear in many of his plays, especially in *Sanyasi* ("Nature's Revenge"), *Phalguni* ("The Cycle of Spring"), and *Mukta-dhara* ("Free Current"). In some of his dramas he introduced the character of the Blind Singer (reminiscent of the Vivek) who sings on behalf of the characters, comments on life, and warns the people of the coming events. The two actor-directors Utpal Dutt and Sombu Mitra are using some Jatra techniques in their productions. The leading choreographer Uday Shankar, pioneer of modern Indian Ballet, has utilized folk rhythms, costumes, masks, dances, and postures. His junior colleague, Shanti Bardhan, created a superb ballet, *India Immortal*, for the Indian People's Theater Association—a galvanizing force in the forties. It spread as a left-wing movement all over India exploiting folk tunes, rhythms, dances, and theatrical conventions which broke down the wall between the audience and the player. In 1952, Shanti Bardhan founded the Little Ballet Troupe in Bombay and produced his famous dance-drama *The Ramayana*. The characters wore masks and moved with stiff, puppetlike movements. Intuitively linked with the best contemporary stage, Bardhan made ballet history with his puppet dance-drama imbued with folk tradition. Narendra Sharma, director of Bharatiya Kala Kendra, a ballet center in New Delhi, produced a spectacular Ramlila on an open-air stage in 1957, combining classical and folk dances. This production has become an annual feature of the capital.

In Hindi, new writers like Dharam Vir Bharati and Mohan Rakesh are conscious of the relationship of the folk and the classical. Habib Tanvir, who studied the latest trends during his years in Europe, directed the fourth-century Sanskrit play *Mrichhakatika* ("The Little Clay Cart") without curtains, props, or sets for the Hindustani Theater in 1959. He even imported six tribal players in order to achieve an authentic folk coloring and called his production Nai Nautanki (new Nautanki). In Sanskrit plays, scenic division is absent and action moves from one place to another in a continuous time sequence. The living tradition of folk theater has the same freedom of time and place. Tanvir used it effectively in staging the classical masterpiece. Dina Gandhi and Jayashankar Sundari in Gujarat have championed the Bhavai form and explored its rich heritage. In the Kannada language, Shivaram Karanth has written new operas based on the Yakshagana tradition. In the state of Maharashtra, G. D. Madgulkar and P. L. Deshpande have given a new status to the much-despised Tamasha. In the Punjabi language, Sheila Bhatia, a writer-composer, aided by Snehlata Sanyal, an actress-singer, produced *Heer Ranjha*, an opera inspired by folk melodies and the legendary love story of the beautiful Heer and the handsome Ranjha. It injected energy into the Punjabi theater.

Today folk theater is beginning to be viewed as a form with potentialities. The folk actors consider their theater a ritual. It expresses what is deep-rooted in the people. Folk melodies have revolutionized musical composition; cave drawings have lent simplicity and force to modern painting; primitive hunt mimes have brought a new concept to the ballet; tribal sculpture has lent tension to the sculpture of our time. Folk drama, which provides a many-faceted delight for the spectators, can add color, richness, and vitality to the contemporary theater.

Muria girls beat the ground rhythmically with sticks. In the background their male partners in bison-horn headdresses play on drums. Photograph by Dr. Verrier Elwin

GLOSSARY

A Muria bison-horn dancer. Photograph by Dr. Verrier Elwin

ABHINAYA: action, gestures expressing a particular emotion.

ADHIKARI: stage manager–director (Jatra).

AKHARA: wrestling pit or arena; in folk theater, school of acting.

ALAAP: introductory elaboration of notes of a classical melody sung without words or beat to evoke the spirit of the melody.

ANU-PALLAVI: second part of a song (Therukoothu).

ARATI: offering of a prayer while waving worship lamps before the image of the god.

ARDHANARISHWARA: the form of Shiva as half male and half female.

ARTHADHARI: actors who expound the meaning of the drama, emphasizing the literary and metaphysical interpretation, rather than expressing it through acting (Tala Maddale). See also VESHADHARI.

ASAR: arena stage (Jatra).

ASHRAM: hermitage.

ATIMA: prayer sung at the end of a play.

AVAHAN: the invoking of a deity.

BAITHAK: large sitting room.

BANKA: young boy dressed to display opulent costumes and jewelry in the procession of Ramlila at Varanasi.

BEHALA: violin (Jatra).

BEHAR-E-TWEEL: lengthy metrical composition used for narrative singing (Nautanki).

BHAGAVATHA: literally, man of God; stage manager–singer in a religious play, as in Yakshagana, Kuchipudi, or Bhagavatha Mela.

BHAINT: devotional song.

BHAKTI: devotion. A religious movement that advocated worship of the god through devotion. It reached one of its peaks in the sixteenth century.

BHAVA: feeling, emotion. According to the Natyasastra, the two-thousand-year-old sacred book of Hindu dramaturgy, these are eight in number: love (rati), laughter (hasya), sorrow (shoka), anger (krodha), energy (utsaha), fear (bhaya), disgust (jugupsa), and astonishment (vismaya). See also RASA.

BHOG: offering of food to the deity.

BHUNGAL: five-foot-long copper wind instrument used in the Bhavai.

BURRA: hollowed pumpkin.

CHACHAR: round arena stage (Bhavai).

CHAKKAR: whirling movement of a dancer.

CHALI: style of walk.

CHANDE: barrel-shaped drum which produces a sharp, piercing clatter; used in Kathakali and Yakshagana.

CHARANAM: literally, feet; the last part of a song (Therukoothu).

CHARNAMIT, CHARNAMRIT: a mixture of milk, fruits, and spices which the temple priest offers to the deity. He then gives a spoonful of this consecrated "nectar" to the devotee, who receives it in cupped hands and sips it.

CHAUBOLA: four-line verse in the Nautanki.

CHAVADI: meeting place for the villagers where they get together to gossip, smoke, and settle their problems (Yakshagana).

CHHABI: picture or image; in Raslila performances, a tableau suddenly revealed to the devotee audiences.

CHOORIDAR: trousers, generally of white cotton, which bulge above the knees and cling from the knees down, forming gathers at the ankles.

DAKSHINA: fee for a Brahmin invited for dinner or to officiate at a religious function.

DARU: musical composition in slow rhythm suited for interpretative acting.

DHAMSA: large kettledrum.

DHOLAK: horizontal drum.

DHRUPAD: classical music composition elaborating the melody and sung majestically and in slow rhythm.

DHUN: melody.

DOHA: couplet.

GANA: abbreviation of Ganesha; in Tamasha, invocation song in praise of Ganesha.

GAULAN: milkmaid. The Tamasha woman acts this role and serves almost the same function as the Sutradhara's wife in the opening of a classical Sanskrit drama.

GHUNGAT: veil, generally the sari or a shawl pulled down over the face.

GOPI: a milkmaid, female friend, and devotee of the god in the cult of Krishna.

GOPURAM: tower over the main entrance of a South Indian temple.

GUMMAT: performing troupe (Tamasha).

GURU: teacher.

HALGI: drum with a fierce loud noise used in Tamasha. It is made of the skin of a goat's belly tightly mounted on one side of a wooden hoop, with the other side left hollow.

HANUMANAYAKA: Clown (Yakshagana).

HASTA: hand gesture in the classical dance.

INDRADHWAJA: Indra's staff. See also JARJARA.

JANIYAU: sacred thread worn by a Hindu. It passes over his left shoulder across his chest and down to his waist on the right side.

JARJARA: the god Indra's flagstaff, which was used in the first dramatic production in the heavens to drive away the evil spirits. Later it became an essential element of the stage preliminaries.

JURI: literally, double. A set of singers who sang on behalf of the characters in the nineteenth-century Jatra.

KAKRA: a twisted cloth soaked in oil and tightly rolled so that when lighted at one end it burns steadily like a torch. Female characters brandish these torches when they enter and dance (Bhavai).

KANCHALIYA: female character dancer in Bhavai, so-called because she wears a kanchali (blouse).

KARANA: dance pose with a specific posture of hands and legs.

KATAN: triple blaze of rhythmic beats that serves as a transfer from one song to another in Chhau dance-drama.

KATTIAKARAN: herald who maintains order. In Therukoothu folk theater, he carries out the duties of stage manager and director.

KEERTAN: religious singing in which the principal devotee sings and the congregation joins him.

KHARTAL: wooden clappers studded with brass rings and held in the singer's hands.

KOMALI: Buffoon (Therukoothu).

KONANGI: Buffoon (Bhagavatha Mela).

KUTILAKA: S-shaped stick carried by the Buffoon.

LASYA: lyrical and graceful element in the dance. See also TANDAVA.

LAVANI: narrative poetical composition with a special melodic form that has heroic vigor (Tamasha).

LEHNGA: loose, flowing skirt.

LILA: sport, the divine purpose of creating the world according to the Vedantic philosophy; a play.

LINGA, LINGAM: phallic symbol used as an abstract representation of Shiva.

MADDALE, MADDALAM: long horizontal drum.

MAHURI: type of flute used in Chhau dance-drama.

MANDALI: troupe of actors.

MANGALACHARANA: prayer song.

MANJEERA: tiny metal cymbals.

MANTRA: verse, phrase, or hymn believed to have spiritual powers when chanted.

MAUND: Indian weight equivalent to eighty-two pounds.

MELA: performing troupe.

MRIDANGAM: horizontal drum used in classical dances. It has a rich vocabulary of rhythms and sound syllables.

MUNDASU: giant turban worn by the heroic character (Yakshagana).

NAGMA: musical composition of a devotional nature, sung with a repeated refrain that arouses ecstasy in the singers and listeners (Nautanki and Bhand Jashna).

NAIK: director.

NARGHAN: pair of small vertical drums which the Bhavai instrumentalist ties around his waist and plays while standing.

NATAK: drama.

NATI: actress; wife of the stage manager.

NAYIKA: heroine. In classical dance aesthetics, there are eight primary kinds of nayika in different emotional situations, three primary kinds according to age, and three further primary kinds according to character and social position.

NAUTCH: dance generally associated with singing girls.

NIRGUNA: philosophical term referring to God as an abstract entity with no physical manifestation.

ORHNI: shawl worn by women in Gujarat. It covers the head, and one end is tucked in at the waist.

PAINÐIA: club-footed, mischievous character who accompanies the Buffoon in Tamasha and fusses over everything.

PAKHAWAJ: horizontal drum.

PALA: Jatra play, operatic in character.

PALLAVI: refrain of a song; its opening part (Therukoothu).

PAN: betel leaf.

PANDAL: improvised auditorium constructed of temporary materials.

PARIKHANDA: popular war exercise in which the soldiers use *pari* (shield) and *khanda* (sword). The steps are used in the Chhau dance and are characterized by vigor and split-second timing.

PAUDH: round arena stage (Bhavai).

PICHHVAI: backdrop (Raslila).

PRASANGA: play characterized by a great deal of logical argument and philosophical discussion through which the actors expound its meaning.

PRASHAD: food offered to a deity and thus sanctified to be distributed among the devotees.

PUJA: worship.

PURANAS: massive collection of myths, legends, traditional history of the universe and its creation, and stories of religious guidance (fifth to eighth century A.D.). There are eighteen major ones, of which *Shrimad Bhagavata Purana* is one of the most important.

PURVARANGA: ceremonies before the main play starts.

PUSHP-VIMAN: flower-decked aerial vehicle that carried Rama to Ayodhya after he had defeated Ravana.

QAWALI: type of singing in which a group of singers clap their hands and sway their heads in ecstasy. The principal singer leads, and the others join in the refrain. Love songs and religious philosophical poetry are popular in this form.

RAGA: melodic mode. A large variety of these form the repertoire of Indian classical music.

RAGINI: ramification of the principal *raga*, sung in classical form.

RANGA: stage; in Bhavai, the stage manager.

RASA: sentiment. Corresponding to the *bhava*, these are eight in number: erotic (*sringara*), comic (*hasya*), pathetic (*karuna*), furious (*raudra*), heroic (*vira*), terrible (*bhayanaka*), odious (*bibhatsa*), marvelous (*adbhuta*).

RAS ASTHAN: acting area in Raslila plays.

RUDRAKSHAMALA: rosary of beads sacred to Shiva.

RUPEE: Indian monetary unit. One American dollar is equal to approximately 4.75 rupees.

SADHU: monk, hermit.

SANGEET: music.

SARANGI: wooden instrument with gut strings, played with a bow.

SEER: Indian weight equivalent to slightly more than two pounds.

SETH: rich man.

SHAKTI: the Goddess of Power, Kali, the creative female energy.

SHASTRAS: scriptures; ancient books on religion, philosophy, love, politics, and other subjects written by saints and philosophers and invoked as authorities.

SHLOKA: couplet.

SINGHASAN: throne; in Raslila, the cushioned divan on which Krishna and Radha sit. It is set on a platform a foot higher than the acting area.

SONGADYA: Buffoon impersonating Krishna in Tamasha.

SUTRADHARA: stage manager—director in classical Sanskrit drama.

SWAMI: leader of the Raslila troupe who acts as the principal singer and director.

TALA: time, beat, rhythm (in music and dance).

TALAM: tiny metallic cymbals used to give the beat.

TANDAVA: heroic and furious element in the dance. See also LASYA.

THEKAWALI: temporarily organized group of players (Jatra).

THIRAI CHEELAI: length of white cloth used as a hand curtain in Therukoothu. The principal characters are introduced on the stage from behind this curtain.

THUMRI: classical style of singing in which the sensuous and delicate elements of the melody are emphasized.

TIHAI: three-fold repetition of drum syllables in a sequence which the dancer executes by his footwork at the conclusion of a dance sequence.

TORAH: sequence of rhythmic drum syllables.

TRISHUL: trident, the chief weapon of the god Shiva.

TUNTUNA: one-stringed wooden instrument (Tamasha).

UPALAYA: style of walk combined with bodily movements to form an expressive action. Upalayas make up the basic vocabulary in Chhau dance.

VAG: main play (Tamasha).

VAISHNAVA: religious movement centering around Rama and Krishna as the principal incarnations of the god Vishnu. It produced many saint-poets who composed superb devotional poetry and popularized the movement.

VANDANA: opening prayer song in a play.

VESHA: dress, role; in Bhavai, a playlet.

VESHADHARI: literally, one who puts on costumes and make-up; actors who interpret the character by using all the theatrical devices. Contrasted with ARTHADHARI.

VIRUTHAM: verse sung without rhythmic accompaniment.

VIVEK: conscience, discrimination; an important character in the Jatra. He sings out the inner conflict of a character, acts as his double, warns or guides him by a song, or comments on future events.

VYAS: stage manager—director in the Ramlila plays in Varanasi. Vyas, the great bard who wrote the Mahabharata, was said to have an all-knowing eye and mind.

YAGNA: sacrificial ceremony performed to propitiate the gods.

YAKSHA: celestial being, a class of demigod.

YAKSHI: female yaksha.

YOGI: ascetic.

INDEX

Abhinaya (expressive miming), 20,
162; forms of, 192
Actresses: male, 21–23, 43, 49, 53,
69, 75, 98–99, 128, 175, 192;
female, 21–23, 34, 46–47, 49,
63, 75, 81–82, 150, 187, 194
Adhikari, Badan, 15
Adhikari, Sisuram, 15
Adhikari (Stage Manager), 16
Aharya, 192. See also Abhinaya
Ahirs, 104
Ahmedabad, 51, 70, 131
Akbar the Great, 116, 170, 185.
See also Moghul
Akhara (school), 43, 46, 47, 130,
179. See also Nautanki
Alaap, 136, 148
Alwal (village), 189
Amanat, Agha Hassan (Urdu
poet), 42
Amar Singh Rathaur, 39, 48
Amba Mata (Goddess of Power),
51, 54, 61, 67, 68, 71
Ambedkar, Dr., 74
Amriteshwari (goddess), 162
Amriteshwari Mela, 162
Andhra, 21, 183, 187, 189, 197
Angika, 192. See also Abhinava
Ankia Nat (one-act play), 118,
183, 185
Anno, 44
Antima, 154
Aram Raj, 70–71
Arasur (worship center), 51
Arati, 109, 122; play "Offering of
Light," 173
Archi-chali, 178
Ardhanarishwara (form of Shiva),
167, 171. See also Shiva
Ardhanarishwara (play), 67
Arthadhari, 163
Arya Bhushan Theater, 85
Asaita. See Thakar, Asaita
Asar (stage), 11, 18, 27
Ashram, 108
Ashta Chhap (group of poets),
116, 118, 125, 195
Ashwin Poornima (festival), 108
Asi (stream), 92
Assam, 4, 31, 115, 117, 183, 195
Astradanda ("Sword Play"), 173
Audichya (clan), 51
Aurangzeb (Moghul emperor),
21, 73
Avahan. See Gana

Babajan, 49
Bahucharaji (goddess), 51, 67
Bajirao I, 73
Bajirao II, 73, 75
Bala, 75

Balaji, 48
Balatripura-sundari (goddess), 191
Bale-Ghati (lavani), 81
Balmokand, Guru, 49
Banaras. See Varanasi
Banarsi, Raunaq, 112
Banaviddha ("The Arrowstruck
Deer"), 173
Banglar Bodhu ("The Bride of
Bengal"), 20, 30
Bangriposi Hills, 167
Banka, 105–6
Bannerjee, Hiralal, 31
Bapat, Vasant, 88
Bardai, Chand, 119
Bardhan, Shanti, 199
Bardwan (city), 31–32
Bargi Elo Deshe ("The Maratha
Invasion of Bengal"), 20, 30
Baripada District, 180
Barkur (village), 160
Baroda (city), 51
Barsana (village), 115
Baul (singer), 199
Bawa ("The Monk"), 61
Bayabai, 74
Bayalata, 163
Bayal-nataka, 188
Bazar Shahi Akhara, 179
Behar-e-tweel, 38
Belgaum, 163
Bengal, 6, 13, 15, 31, 115–17, 199
Betel, 59, 92
Bhagat, 46–47. See also Nautanki
Bhagat, Megha, 94
Bhagavad Gita, 115, 131
Bhagavata Purana, 131
Bhagavatha, 4, 20, 27, 145, 147–
48, 150–54, 157–60, 164,
191, 193–94
Bhagavatha Mela, 135, 137, 170,
183, 192–93
Bhagavathi (goddess), 162
Bhagyachandra, Maharaja, 118
Bhaint (invocation song), 37, 47
Bhakta, 117, 168
Bhakti movement, 14
Bhand, 185
Bhand Jashna, 183, 186
Bhand Pather, 186
Bhanja, Upendra, 179
Bharata Milap, 104
Bharata Natyam (dance), 86, 192
Bharati, Dharam Vir, 199
Bharatiya Kala Kendra (ballet
center), 199
Bhatia, Sheila, 200
Bhatiali (folk tune), 28
Bhatt, Narayan, 119
Bhatt, Shree, 128
Bhatta, Rama, 160